Redemption That Liberates

Redemption That Liberates
Political Theologies of Richard Mouw and Nam-dong Suh

Wonho Jung

☙PICKWICK *Publications* • Eugene, Oregon

REDEMPTION THAT LIBERATES
Political Theologies of Richard Mouw and Nam-dong Suh

Copyright © 2018 Wonho Jung. All rights reserved. Except for brief quotations in critical publications or reviews, no part of this book may be reproduced in any manner without prior written permission from the publisher. Write: Permissions, Wipf and Stock Publishers, 199 W. 8th Ave., Suite 3, Eugene, OR 97401.

Pickwick Publications
An Imprint of Wipf and Stock Publishers
199 W. 8th Ave., Suite 3
Eugene, OR 97401

www.wipfandstock.com

PAPERBACK ISBN: 978-1-5326-1813-0
HARDCOVER ISBN: 978-1-5326-4014-8
EBOOK ISBN: 978-1-5326-4015-5

Cataloguing-in-Publication data:

Names: Jung, Wonho, author.

Title: Redemption that liberates : political theologies of Richard Mouw and Nam-dong Suh / Wonho Jung.

Description: Eugene, OR : Pickwick Publications, 2018 | Includes bibliographical references.

Identifiers: ISBN 978-1-5326-1813-0 (paperback) | ISBN 978-1-5326-4014-8 (hardcover) | ISBN 978-1-5326-4015-5 (ebook)

Subjects: LCSH: Mouw, Richard J. | Suh, Namdong. | Christian ethics. | Calvinism. | Minjung theology. | Liberty—Religious aspects—Christianity. | Redemption.

Classification: BS511.2 .J86 2018 (print) | BS511.2 .J86 (ebook)

Manufactured in the U.S.A. 02/07/18

Unless otherwise noted, all Scripture quotations are from the New Revised Standard Version Bible, copyright © 1989, Division of Christian Education of the National Council of the Churches of Christ in the United States of America. Used by permission. All rights reserved.

To
Caleb, Daniel, Olivia,
and Mimi

Contents

Preface | ix

1. Introduction | 1
2. A Preliminary Survey of Minjung Theology | 17
3. A Preliminary Survey of the Neo-Calvinist Worldview | 35
4. The *Both/And* Way of Thinking | 61
5. Anthropological Comparison: What Is the Human Problem? | 64
6. Christological Comparison: Who Is Jesus? | 86
7. Eschatological Comparison: What Is the Kingdom of God? | 120
8. Crossroad of the Two Theologies | 143
9. Conclusion | 155

Bibliography | 159

Preface

THIS BOOK MARKS AN essential milestone on my theological journey. It reflects my pursuit of a Reformed vision of social transformation that is theologically more coherent and politically more responsible. Raised in a Reformed Christian tradition, I detected that *orthodoxy* has not always been accompanied by *orthopraxis*. Further, it was perplexing to see that many self-identified evangelical Christians (and even ministers and theologians) uncritically endorsed conservative political ideology as if it was biblically warranted. Anxious for socially responsible Christian practice, I joined a social justice ministry of a minjung (the poor) church in a slum on the outskirts of Seoul, while studying Christian ethics in a graduate school.

My experience of the minjung church movement was characterized by mixed feelings of fulfillment and uneasiness. It confirmed my belief that Christians must become actively and responsibly involved in endeavors for sociopolitical transformation in order to live out their faith and to love their neighbors, who are not only spiritual but also social and political beings. On the other hand, the theology that inspired the movement did not seem to be adequately consistent with my Reformed conviction. The liberation that they advocated was not radical enough to deal with all dimensions of human alienation, which include distortions in both social and spiritual relationships. A liberation-oriented theology that disregards the spiritual dimension of salvation and a redemption-oriented theology that overlooks the social dimension of salvation have been unable to achieve a constructive dialogue with the other and are far less capable of successfully persuading the other because they both have a critical flaw that the other is very well aware of. We need a redemption that liberates and a liberation that redeems. Our understanding of redemption or liberation should be so comprehensive as to cover all aspects of human problems; it should also produce a more adequate theological vision of social transformation that remedies the pervasive dualism between the personal and the social, the spiritual and the political, and the this-worldly and the other-worldly. This is where my project in this book begins.

In writing this book I am indebted to so many people that I cannot name them all here. This makes me humbled. But I'd like to mention the one person who has been most influential to me and to my project, the person who is true human and true God. His lordship over everything gave me confidence in understanding his redemptive work as reaching every sphere of life including political life. If there is anything in this book that contributes to the genuine understanding of what Christ has done, is doing, and calls his followers to do in his redemptive activity, I will say that it was done through the enlightenment and empowerment by his Spirit. It is also my hope that any errors or weak points that this book may contain can be used to further the theological conversation that promotes his kingdom.

1

Introduction

Problem and Argument

MINJUNG THEOLOGY IS A revolutionary theological idea that was developed in the military dictatorial regime in South Korea during the 1970s. It has provided a tool for interpreting history and society from a biblical perspective and has inspired a social transformation movement among progressive Christians. Minjung theology, utilizing the sociohistorical analysis of the life of the minjung (oppressed people), identifies the minjung as the powerless who are economically exploited, socially alienated, and politically oppressed and advocates their liberation from such dehumanizing conditions. Arguably the most prominent theological contribution from Korean Christianity, minjung theology, however, has faced severe criticisms, especially from Korean Reformed theologians. Central to these criticisms are debates about minjung Christology.

Byung-mu Ahn, one of the most influential minjung theologians, contends that christological titles of the Western traditional theology such as Messiah, the Lord, Son of God, and Son of Man cannot be exclusively applied to Jesus of Nazareth.[1] He also rejects the traditional doctrine of Jesus' two natures.[2] For him, Christ should be understood not as an individual person but as a messianic *event* or messianic *movement* of the minjung for their own liberation.[3] Because he regards Jesus as a collective symbol for the

---

1. Ahn, *Discourse on Minjung Theology*, 97.
2. Ibid., 87.
3. Ahn, *Galilean Jesus*, 36. In a similar vein, Yong-bock Kim calls resistant movements of the oppressed people in Korean history, such as the Donghak Peasant Revolution, messianic movements. Not surprisingly, therefore, he names Jae-woo Choi, the leader of the Donghak Peasant Revolution, Messiah Choi or Jesus Choi. See Yong-bock Kim, "Messiah and the Minjung," 294–95.

minjung, Ahn argues that it was not Jesus of Nazareth but rather the minjung who were rejected, unjustly tried, and crucified by the powers that be.[4] In the same way, what the biblical report of the empty tomb event signifies is, according to him, the resurrection of the Galilean minjung rather than that of the historical person Jesus.[5] Overall, he and other minjung theologians criticize Western traditional theology in general, and Nicene and Chalcedonian Christology in particular, as a system of religious dogma that supports the status quo for the ruling class.

Theologians with traditional Christology, especially in the Reformed theological tradition, have then vigorously criticized minjung theology, raising serious doubts about whether it can be regarded as a Christian theology from any Orthodox Christian theological perspective. After examining minjung theologians' interpretation of Jesus in the Gospel narratives, Seyoon Kim concludes that, because of its fatal exegetical inconsistencies, along with its syncretistic and anti-Christian characteristics, minjung theology is no more a Christian theology than Moonism.[6] Another Reformed scholar Eunsoo Kim criticizes minjung theology's methodology as a nonreligious, socioeconomic interpretation of the Scriptures and raises questions concerning the minjung concept of God. According to him, minjung theology rejects the traditional understanding of God as triune and transcendent and thus virtually amounts to an atheistic theology from his Reformed theological perspective.[7]

A voice in minjung theology, however, to which those criticisms cannot aptly apply is that of Nam-dong Suh. Along with Byung-mu Ahn, Suh is one of the two founding fathers of minjung theology and portrays significant differences from Ahn in many theological points. They agree on the decisive role of the minjung in the process of human salvation. In contrast to Ahn, however, Suh does not reject traditional Christology in his articulation of minjung theology but affirms Jesus' unique role as Messiah. His minjung messianism does not identify the minjung as the Messiah in an ontological sense but emphasizes the critical role of the minjung in human salvation. While Ahn understands the crucifixion of Jesus only as a political event, Suh recognizes both political and religious implications of the cross. Considering these observations, Reformed theologians' criticism

---

4. Ahn, "Subject of History," 183.
5. Ibid., 184.
6. Seyoon Kim, "Is 'Minjung Theology,'" 272–73.
7. Eunsoo Kim, "Minjung Theology in Korea," 55, 58.

of minjung theology as a non-Christian or atheist theology is not applicable at least to Nam-dong Suh's rendition of minjung theology.

Another vision of social transformation in the Korean church is called the neo-Calvinist worldview or the Christian worldview.[8] Minjung theology and the neo-Calvinist worldview are the two revolutionary theological ideas that inspired recent social transformation movements in Korea, the minjung church movement and the Christian worldview movement, respectively. Both were called "movement" because their moral visions were directed toward stimulating responsible social engagement among Christians and effecting a practical transformation in a larger society. The redemptive vision of the neo-Calvinist worldview, introduced to Korean Christians in the early 1980s, is anchored in the biblical motifs of *creation–fall–redemption–consummation* as a methodological tool to interpret history and society, with its pivotal claim being that Christ's redemptive activity and sovereignty reach all areas of life that have fallen from the original order of creation.

Despite their comparable visions of social transformation informed by theological perspectives, minjung theology and the neo-Calvinist worldview have been generally considered theologically incompatible. While Reformed theologians criticize minjung theology as unwarrantedly politicized, minjung theologians criticize the Reformed social vision as fatally lacking the structural approach to social evil. According to Hyung-mook Choi, one of the most active contemporary minjung theologians, even the evangelicals who seek social transformation as an essential Christian mission show an individualistic tendency in their approach.[9] They naively believe that a change in the individual heart will bring about social change and do not pay adequate attention to the problem of structural injustice. For Choi, this is the limitation of the Christian worldview movement that

---

8. Certainly people of different theological traditions and convictions hold different Christian worldviews, the neo-Calvinist worldview, often called the "Reformed world and life view," being one of them. In the introduction of the neo-Calvinist worldview discussions into the Korean church and its development into the Christian worldview movement, however, the neo-Calvinist worldview was translated into Korean simply as "Christian worldview" and used in such phrases as "Christian worldview seminar," "Christian worldview school," and "Christian worldview movement." Thus, when the term "Christian worldview" is used in Korean, in most cases it refers to the neo-Calvinist worldview. In this study, unless otherwise indicated, "Christian worldview" and "Reformed world and life view" refer to the neo-Calvinist worldview shaped by Abraham Kuyper and his followers on the ground of the theologies of Augustine and John Calvin.

9. Choi, "Critical Remarks," paras. 12–14.

has made minjung theologians suspicious of whether the Reformed transformational vision can actually effect social change.

Richard Mouw sympathizes with this critique and offers an alternative perspective. A Reformed theologian himself, Mouw is not persuaded by the evangelical belief that to change the individual heart is to change society. Rather, he argues that a political approach to social transformation is crucial because injustice is structurally and systemically built into the human social and political relationships.[10] Developing his political theology from the neo-Calvinist worldview, Mouw understands political activities and relationships in the light of *creation–fall–redemption–consummation* and maintains that redemption in Christ should involve the transformation of unjust political order. Considering this, the criticism by minjung theologians of Western theology in general as apolitical, status-quo theology and Reformed theology specifically as tending toward pietistic individualism in its social approach cannot be reasonably directed toward Mouw's neo-Calvinist political theology.

For many Korean Reformed theologians and Christians, Mouw's approach has seemed to be a constructive challenge to the Korean church, which is dominantly conservative in its approach to social and political concerns. Since the late 1980s, most of his books have been translated into Korean, and he is considered the spokesperson for the Reformed model of social transformation. According to Wonha Shin, a Calvinist ethicist of a Korean Reformed seminary, Mouw, like mainstream ethicists, emphasizes social transformation as a Christian mission and seeks it through active political involvement, but unlike them he grounds his political ethic on scriptural authority.[11] This makes his political theology characteristically Reformed and, at the same time, open to dialog with other approaches of public theology. In this regard, Shin appreciates Mouw's pursuit of a "softer Calvinism" because in this approach "the traditional Calvinistic rigidity is removed and a learning dialog with other traditions is encouraged."[12]

This openness of Mouw's political ethic, however, has not yet fully extended to a learning dialog with minjung theology. As discussed above, Reformed criticism of minjung theology cannot be fittingly applied to Nam-dong Suh's articulation of minjung theology and minjung theologians' criticism of the Reformed theology cannot be aptly directed to

10. Mouw, *Politics and Biblical Drama*, 49–50; Mouw, *When the Kings Come*, 64.
11. Won Ha Shin, "Two Models," 185–86.
12. Ibid., 193.

INTRODUCTION

Mouw's political theology. On the contrary, Nam-dong Suh shows a possible way of doing minjung theology without necessarily rejecting what some theologians argue to be essential elements of Reformed Christology. Richard Mouw, on the other hand, radically and consistently applies the neo-Calvinist worldview to the discussion of politics and shows openness to a similar focus on structural and political change as do minjung theologians. Further, the essential themes of the political theologies of Suh and Mouw show a significant affinity with each other. The central discussions of Suh's liberation-oriented theology involve the themes of the fundamental human problem, the Messiah as the agent of liberation, and the kingdom of God as the end of the liberation, and these themes find a parallel in Mouw's neo-Calvinist discussion of politics.

This study will compare Nam-dong Suh's formulation of minjung theology and Richard Mouw's neo-Calvinist political theology in terms of each theology's treatment or understanding of the human problem, Christology, and the kingdom of God. Based on the comparative observations of the two theological visions, the current study will argue that, contrary to the criticisms of Reformed and minjung theologians against each other, Suh's minjung theology and Mouw's neo-Calvinist political theology are compatible with each other with respect to the salient points of anthropological, christological, and eschatological discussions. This compatibility, then, can suggest a possible way of reconciling the two transformational visions of minjung theology and the neo-Calvinist worldview for a theologically more cogent and socially more relevant vision of transformation for Korean society.

Method and Limitations

This study examines how Nam-dong Suh's minjung theology and Richard Mouw's Reformed political theology correspond with each other and how they might mutually enrich one another. Unlike other minjung theologians, Suh recognizes traditional Christology while holding firmly the distinctive tenets of minjung theology. This makes his approach unique among minjung theologians. Mouw criticizes socially and politically unconcerned theologies as inadequate and puts a strong emphasis on Christian engagement for social justice based on his radical understanding of the Reformed faith. He extends the Reformed concern of the fundamental redemption in Christ into the area of human political relationships and this makes his approach distinctive in Reformed theology. Despite the above-described criticisms between minjung and Reformed theologians against each other, therefore, a carefully constructed theological comparison between Suh and Mouw will show that a creative conversation between minjung and Reformed theologies is possible for a more constructive Christian social vision. It is with this expectation that the current study choose to discuss Suh's minjung theology and Mouw's Reformed political theology with the focus on their understandings of the theologically envisioned social and political transformation.

Though coming from different theological traditions, Suh and Mouw show considerable affinities with each other in their theological ethics of social transformation. They develop their theological reflections in the *both/and* way of thinking and this is pivotal in comparing their theologies. In contrast to the *either/or* way of thinking, in which two opposite ideas are always mutually exclusive and one has to be chosen over the other, the *both/and* approach takes the two contrary ideas as complementing, instead of rejecting, each other.[13] This inclusive and harmonious way of thinking is prominent in both Suh's and Mouw's theologizing and makes their theologies comparable. Centering on their shared approach, we discuss Suh's minjung theology against the backdrop of Byung-mu Ahn's minjung theology and Mouw's theology against the backdrop of David VanDrunen's Reformed theology. Ahn and Suh share many important ideas in their development of minjung theology, and VanDrunen and Mouw share significant elements of Reformed theology. In contrast to Suh and Mouw, however, Ahn and VanDrunen show the *either/or* way of thinking in their theological discussions. Comparing Suh and Mouw with them, therefore, we can get a clearer understanding of Suh's and Mouw's theologies to show how their theological visions are mutually acceptable.

Suh and Ahn, while largely regarded as the two founding fathers of minjung theology, show notable differences in their articulation of minjung theology. In fact, minjung theology has been developed in a polyphonous way: minjung theologians have presented different understandings on some important issues yet in the name of minjung theology. Such differences can be traced back to Nam-dong Suh and Byung-mu Ahn. The most important difference between these two theological approaches may be the

13. For a discussion of the *both/and* thinking in contrast to the *either/or* thinking, see Jung Young Lee, *Trinity in Asian Perspective*, 24–34; idem, *Marginality*, 69. We will provide a detailed discuss of this holistic way of thinking that Suh and Mouw share later in chapter 4.

way each theologian conceives of his theology. Suh considers his theology a remedy, rather than a replacement, for traditional Western theology, which, according to him, tends to spiritualize and depoliticize the original gospel of liberation for the minjung. Thus, he leaves room for conversation with traditional theology. Ahn, on the contrary, argues for an interpretation of Jesus that is radically different from Chalcedonian Christology. This renders Ahn's theology and any traditionally oriented theology mutually incompatible unless one of the two theologies makes a significant compromise in its principal statements.

In order to provide a clear understanding of Mouw's Reformed political theology, his view will be compared with that of David VanDrunen. A Calvinist theologian of Westminster Seminary in California and one of a number of prominent Reformed critics of neo-Calvinism and Kuyper, VanDrunen argues for a narrow understanding of Christ's redemptive work as limited to personal and spiritual renewal. When compared to his view, which is characteristic of the belief of mainstream Korean Christians, Mouw's theological perspective will show a distinctive approach to social transformation, yet rooted in the same Calvinist tradition. The comparison between Suh's minjung theology and Mouw's Reformed political theology in the backdrop of Ahn's minjung theology and VanDrunen's Reformed theology will demonstrate that, while irreconcilable differences exist between Ahn and VanDrunen in their separate conceptions of the work of Christ, considerable affinities are also present between Suh and Mouw in their approach to theologically informed social transformation and the significance of the work of Christ for this transformation.

Along with the affinities between Suh's and Mouw's political theologies, this comparative study looks for a way in which the two perspectives can challenge each other to suggest a fuller constructive vision of social transformation. It is especially relevant considering the recent stagnation in both the minjung church movement and the Christian worldview movement. Like Mouw, Suh shows a balanced and holistic understanding of the scope of redemption in Christ in opposition to both secularism and sectarianism. Unlike Mouw, however, he tends to understand the church in a parochial sense and downplay its role in social transformation. Mouw's broad understanding of the church and his emphasis on the church as the agent of redemption in Christ, then, can be a constructive challenge to Suh's ecclesiology. In part because his theology is text oriented, with philosophical reflections, Mouw's emphasis on the centrality of the church, on the other hand, tends to weaken active Christian political involvement in solidarity with the oppressed. He shows a more systematic interpretation of the biblically informed vision of social transformation but a less context-sensitive approach to political injustice and social inequality. Suh's theological method of from-context-to-text, then, can present a creative challenge to Mouw for a more sympathetic approach to the life of the oppressed and a more down-to-earth praxis for their liberation.

These differences between Suh and Mouw are more clearly observable when the minjung church movement and the Christian worldview movement are compared. The minjung church movement has separated itself from the traditional church and related itself more with the Korean minjung tradition. The Christian worldview movement, on the other hand, has become more like an intellectualist movement with the aim of developing and disseminating the Christian worldview way of thinking. This, among others, explains why those movements have had little impact on the Korean society and are undergoing recent stagnation. In this respect, the current study is expected not only to provide a more compelling vision of social transformation by comparing Suh's minjung theology and Mouw's Reformed political theology; it is also expected to suggest a renewed and enhanced way of Christian practice for social transformation by looking at a way in which the minjung church movement and the Christian worldview movement can learn from each other and, possibly, cooperate with each other.

This study is not intended to provide an exhaustive comparison between the entire theological thought of Suh and Mouw. Rather, it focuses on the comparison of their theological visions of social transformation and the compatibility of those visions. Therefore, discussions are limited to the topics that are essentially related to the nature of the conceived transformation and, as a result, the following topics are discussed: the identification of the problematic human conditions that call for transformation, the agent of transformation, and the projected goal of transformation.

These topics are crucial for the understanding the main thrust of the two thinkers' social ethics, and they can be addressed in the questions: (1) What is the fundamental human problem? (2) Who is Jesus? (3) What is the kingdom of God? Each question will be discussed for anthropological, christological, and eschatological comparisons, respectively, between Suh's minjung theology and Mouw's neo-Calvinist political theology.

For the analysis of Nam-dong Suh's presentation of minjung theology, his comprehensive works are examined along with selected writings of Byung-mu Ahn and other minjung theologians published in Korean and English, as listed in the selected bibliography. For the understanding of Richard Mouw's neo-Calvinist political theology, this study examines his theological writings and selected works of other scholars that are pertinent to the discussion of the neo-Calvinist worldview.

Current Discussions

The discussions of minjung theology assume the distinction of three generations in the development of minjung theology since its beginning. The first generation of minjung theology (in the 1970s) is characterized by its attempt to reinterpret the biblical narratives through the eyes of the suffering minjung.[14] The second generation of minjung theology (in the 1980s) is distinguished by its adoption of Marxism in interpreting social and economic injustice against the minjung.[15] Finally, the third generation of minjung theology (since 1990s) is identified by the diverse interests among minjung theologians in such problems as globalization and neoliberalism after the end of military dictatorship in Korea.[16]

Current debates in minjung theology evolve around the issue of whether the foundational statements of first-generation minjung theologians are still valid and relevant to the life of the Korean church today as well as to today's social and political situations. On this matter, contemporary minjung theologians are generally divided into two groups.

One group of minjung theologians maintain without revision the principal arguments of first-generation minjung theology, developed especially

---

14. For example, Ahn, "Markan Theology," 5–26; Nam-dong Suh, "Jesus, Church History," 53–68; Kyong-jai Kim, "Minjung," 77–86. These and other major articles of minjung theology in this period were translated into English and compiled in the 1983 book edited by the Commission of Theological Concerns of the Christian Conference of Asia, *Minjung Theology: People as the Subjects of History*.

15. The major works of the second-generation minjung theology include the following: Kang, "Minjung Theological Adoption"; Chang-rak Kim, "Minjung's Struggle for Liberation"; Kang, *Theology of Matter*.

16. Jin-Ho Kim and Hyung-mook Choi are among the most prominent thinkers of the third-generation minjung theology. Their major works include: Jin-Ho Kim, *For a Practical Christianity*, "Minjung as the Subject of History," "Beyond the Exclusivist Ideology of Theology"; Choi, *Social Transformation Movement and Christian Theology*, "Several Issues in Minjung Theological Discussions."

by Byung-mu Ahn. They attempt to reinterpret these arguments in conversation with contemporary philosophy such as poststructuralism. Due to this group of minjung theologians' tendency of anti-theology or post-theology, this group works beyond the traditional boundary of the church and explores ways toward an alternative church or "a church outside of the church" that finds a new field of doing minjung theology in the civil society rather than in the traditional church. A recently published volume with selected writings of Byung-mu Ahn shows this approach.[17] Founding members of the Christian Institute for the Third Ear, such as Jin-Ho Kim, Hyung-mook Choi, and Chang-rak Kim, can be classified as belonging to this group of minjung theologians. Since 1994, the Institute has published *The Era and Minjung Theology*, a journal of minjung theology discussions.

The other group of minjung theologians, such as Tae-soo Yim, Jae-soon Park, and Jin-kwan Kwon, seeks the theological reconstruction of minjung theology without totally abandoning the traditional frameworks of theology. They assume such traditional christological propositions as the two natures of Christ and find the locus of doing minjung theology in the church. The Institute of Minjung Theology fosters this line of minjung theology discussions and has issued since 2000 the quarterly *The Minjung and Theology*. In particular, Tae-soo Yim has drawn attention to the differences between Byung-mu Ahn and Nam-dong Suh's formulations of minjung theology.[18] According to him, Ahn and Suh show different understandings of the minjung's relationship to the Messiah. Pointing out several inconsistencies in Ahn's minjung theology, he contends that Suh's rendering of minjung theology is a more feasible way of doing minjung theology. Yim's contribution to the discussion of minjung theology is that he has underscored the importance of the differences between the two key advocates of minjung theology, which had been long neglected.

Yim, however, did not develop the implications of Suh's minjung theology further into a new way of doing minjung theology, one which needs not be antithetical to the Reformed theological perspective. He still posits minjung theology against traditional Western theology, which he claims to be anti-minjung. After exploring Suh's minjung theology, this study argues that Suh shows a way of doing minjung theology that does not conflict with Reformed theology but rather corresponds with it.

---

17. Yung Suk Kim and Jin-Ho Kim, eds., *Reading Minjung Theology in the Twenty-First Century*.

18. Yim, "Minjung Theology."

INTRODUCTION

With regard to the current discussion of the neo-Calvinist political theology, recent criticisms against the transformationist Reformed worldview are noteworthy. After the peak of a renaissance in the neo-Calvinist worldview discussions in the 1980s, renewed discussion triggered by scholars such as D. G. Hart, Michael Horton, and David VanDrunen has developed. Theologians of the Calvinist tradition, they are critical of the transformationist neo-Calvinist worldview and argue that the neo-Calvinist interpretation of Calvin as a cultural transformationist is misled. VanDrunen, for example, wants to interpret Calvin's social ethic from a perspective of the two kingdoms doctrine and contends that Calvin had a dualistic view of the spheres of life, making categorical distinction between the spiritual kingdom and the civil kingdom.[19] Putting Calvin in opposition to the neo-Calvinist worldview proponents, VanDrunen's writing suggests that Calvin identified the kingdom of Christ only with the church and the redemption in Christ only with spiritual regeneration. According to him, it was Calvin's persistent conviction that, contrary to the neo-Calvinist interpretation, the idea of redemption has nothing to do with cultural activity in the civil kingdom.

In response to this criticism, several writers, such as Timothy Palmer and Jason Lief, took up their pens to defend the neo-Calvinist transformationist position. While reaffirming that Calvin understood Christ's redemptive activity as reaching all areas of created life, those neo-Calvinist writers try to support the idea of all-embracing transformation by pointing out the universal nature of Christ's lordship and the integrated nature of life. Recently, John Cooper, a systematic theologian of Calvin Theological Seminary, recapped the neo-Calvinist view of cultural transformation. Christian witness to the gospel of Jesus, according to him, should entail "reforming culture and promoting justice."[20] In this regard, Richard Mouw has been consistent in applying the transformationist view of neo-Calvinism to the political dimension of human life, from the publication of *Political Evangelism* to his recent book *The Challenges of Cultural Discipleship*.

This study explores how Nam-dong Suh's exposition of minjung theology corresponds with Richard Mouw's neo-Calvinist political theology. While consistently focused on the main themes of minjung theology, Suh shows a possibility of doing minjung theology without necessarily repudiating the traditional Reformed understanding of Christology. This

---

19. VanDrunen, "Two Kingdoms"; idem, *Natural Law and the Two Kingdoms*.
20. Cooper, "Church," 5.

will become clear when he is discussed in comparison with Mouw's neo-Calvinist political theology. In this regard, the current study is expected to shed new light on the implications of Suh's minjung theology, which has not been fully explored in terms of its potential affinity with the neo-Calvinist Reformed theology.

Minjung theology and neo-Calvinist social ethics not only share the transformationist orientation, but they also prompted social reform movements among Korean Christians in the 1980s. Until now, however, no attempt has been made for an appreciative approach, either from minjung theology to the neo-Calvinist theology or the reverse. For this reason, the current study is expected to prove a possibility of the appreciative conversation between the two transformationist theologies. Overall, by showing the affinity between Suh and Mouw's political theologies, this study provides a long-absent reconciling perspective to the contemporary discussion of minjung theology and neo-Calvinist social ethics.

Structure of the Argument

Before we engage in the comparative discussion between Nam-dong Suh's minjung theology and Richard Mouw's neo-Calvinist political theology, two chapters are devoted to preliminary surveys of minjung theology and the neo-Calvinist worldview. Chapter 2 provides an overview of minjung theology to facilitate its comparison with the neo-Calvinist worldview. The definition of the minjung, which is one of the most critical issues in understanding minjung theology, is discussed along with the historical background of minjung theology and its methodology. Criticisms of minjung theology both from the Reformed theologians and those theologians sympathetic to minjung theology are also observed to achieve a more adequate understanding of controversial issues in minjung theology.

In chapter 3 the theological background and the key ideas of the neo-Calvinist worldview are surveyed as Richard Mouw's political theology is essentially grounded in that worldview. Criticisms of the neo-Calvinist worldview from non-transformationist Reformed theologians are also discussed to achieve a clearer understanding of the transformationist nature of the neo-Calvinist worldview.

Armed with these outlines of minjung theology and the neo-Calvinist worldview, we conduct comparisons between Suh's presentation of minjung theology and Mouw's political application of the neo-Calvinist worldview

INTRODUCTION

in terms of their anthropological, christological, and eschatological compatibilities with each other. Our comparisons between Suh and Mouw are grounded on the *both/and* way of theologizing that they share and, therefore, before engaging in the comparisons, chapter 4 explicates the *both/and* way of thinking with its origin in the yin-yang symbolism of the ancient Chinese philosophy.

Chapter 5 makes a comparison of their anthropological ideas with regard to what they conceive of as the fundamental human problem that any coherent theology must address. Nam-dong Suh, like Byung-mu Ahn, contends that what lies in the heart of the human problem is the injustice the minjung have had to suffer in their experiences of economic exploitation, political oppression, and social alienation. Unlike Ahn, however, he does not reject the religious dimension of human alienation. Reflecting from the neo-Calvinist worldview, Mouw traces back to what is regarded as the religious root of the human problem, i.e., the fall, and then proceeds to consider its effect not just on the human soul but on all dimensions of human life. According to him, the essential nature of the human problem is the human fallenness from the God-ordained order of creation, which is reflected in all human relationships that are broken and distorted. Thus, Mouw sees social and political injustice as having a religious root and being essentially subjected to the redemptive work of Christ. In their consideration of the human problem, Suh begins with the exploitative relationship between the powerful and the powerless and Mouw begins with the humanity's fall. This difference, however, shows Suh's radical focus on liberation from social injustice and Mouw's comprehensive approach to all-encompassing redemption in Christ, both of which can not only be reconciled with each other but can also complement each other. Despite this subtle difference in emphasis, Suh and Mouw concur in recognizing both religious and social dimensions of the human problem. This chapter, therefore, concludes that Suh's minjung theology and Mouw's neo-Calvinist political theology are compatible in their theological considerations of the fundamental human problem.

Chapter 6 discusses christological compatibility. The christological question of the being and work of Jesus is addressed from Suh's minjung theological perspective and Mouw's neo-Calvinist theological perspective in order to see in what sense they understand Jesus as the agent of transformation. Suh's understanding of this shows notable difference from Byung-mu Ahn's minjung theological perspective. According to Ahn, Jesus as a person is not the agent of liberation or salvation, but Jesus as a collective symbol of the minjung is; the minjung are the agents of liberation for themselves and, in this sense, the minjung are identified as the Messiah. Suh shares with Ahn the idea of the decisive role of the minjung in the process of salvation, but he differs from Ahn in that he never denies the traditional understanding of Jesus as being the Messiah in a unique sense. His minjung messianism is an affirmation of the minjung's crucial *role* in salvation rather than their ontological identification as the Messiah. While Ahn accepts only the political implications of the crucifixion of Jesus, Suh does not deny its religious significance. What he contends is that the traditional theology of historic Christianity has limited the scope of the redemption only to religious and personal life. In this regard, we can find a parallel between his view and Mouw's political exposition of the neo-Calvinist worldview.

In the neo-Calvinist worldview, Jesus is the Messiah and the redeemer in an exclusive way, and his redemptive work involves renewing everything that is under the distorting influence of the fall. Christ's redemption, then, is understood as reclaiming the originally good order of creation in all areas of life, including social, political, and economic relationships. Based on this worldview, Mouw views political order not as essentially demonic or merely remedial for a fallen society but as an intrinsic part of God's original order of creation for human life. He argues that it is part of the redemptive work of Christ to restore the political order as intended in creation. Both Suh's minjung theology and Mouw's neo-Calvinist political theology take the redemptive work of Jesus as the foundation of social transformation. They also concur with each other in recognizing the significance of human cooperation in the divine scheme of salvation for the world.

There is a difference in their understanding of the role of the church in effecting the redemption to the world. Mouw holds that the church as the people of God plays an essential role in the redemptive transformation while Suh emphasizes God's liberating activity beyond the boundary of the church. These two different emphases on the particularity or the universality of divine activity, however, need not rule out each other but can counterbalance each other for a more dynamic and holistic understanding of liberation. This chapter, therefore, asserts that Suh's minjung theology and Mouw's neo-Calvinist political theology do not preclude, but in fact can accommodate, each other's perspective with regard to the being and the work of Jesus as the foundation of the transforming vision.

INTRODUCTION

In chapter 7 the eschatological compatibility between the two theological perspectives is discussed. For the present study, discussion of the eschaton is especially relevant because it shows how each perspective conceives of the final goal of transformation. This in turn clarifies how each perspective understands the nature of the kingdom of God. In contrast to Byung-mu Ahn's purely political interpretation of the kingdom of God, Suh maintains that the kingdom of God is more than what a successful political revolution can bring about. His thinking of the kingdom of God keeps the balance between the eschatology within history and the eschatology beyond it. Similarly, Mouw contends that there is continuity between creation and new creation and that the kingdom of God in eschaton is not an entirely new order but an ultimate completion of the kingdom of God that already began and is progressing in history. Both Mouw and Suh work from an integrated perspective on history and eschatology, which recognizes the continuity between the social transformation in history and the transformation in the eschatological kingdom. Regarding the completion of the kingdom of God, Suh puts more emphasis on the human moral accountability and Mouw on the divine initiative. In doing so, however, they do not deny the other's point, and their different emphasis, in fact, can challenge and enhance each other's point. This chapter, therefore, shows that there is an undeniable agreement between Suh's minjung theology and Mouw's neo-Calvinist political theology in their understanding of the kingdom of God and the final goal of transformation.

The overall observation of the main chapters of this study indicates that there are unmistakable agreements between Suh's rendition of minjung theology and Mouw's neo-Calvinist political theology with regard to their visions of social transformation. Their understandings of the essential human problem, the messiahship of Jesus, and the nature of the kingdom of God show that, contrary to the common assumptions, the two theological perspectives do not necessarily rule out each other.

Chapter 8 discusses their theological compatibility based on their implementation of a *both/and* approach in contrast to an *either/or* approach. Implications of the theological affinities between Suh and Mouw for a possible way of renewing the minjung church movement and the Christian worldview movement are also discussed. According to the *both/and* or holistic approach of Suh and Mouw, the Christian worldview movement can challenge the politically inclined interpretation of liberation in the minjung church movement; the minjung church movement, in turn, can challenge the vestiges of dualism and the intellectualist tendency in the Christian worldview movement. Based on these observations, this chapter suggests a more viable theological vision and practice for the transformation of the Korean society.

In the final chapter, a summary of the current project is provided with the conclusion that Nam-dong Suh's exposition of minjung theology and Richard Mouw's neo-Calvinist political theology correspond to each other in their salient points of a theological vision of social transformation. With this conclusion, the present study suggests that the exclusivist criticisms of both minjung theology and the Reformed theology against each other should be reconsidered. Further, it proposes that there is a possible way of appreciating minjung theology from the Reformed theological perspective, and vice versa, for a more feasible way of conceiving a theological vision of social transformation that combines the personal and the social, the spiritual and the political, and the ultimate and the penultimate.

2

A Preliminary Survey of Minjung Theology

Historical Development of Minjung Theology

MINJUNG THEOLOGY WAS NOT born out of theological reflections of some inquisitive armchair theologians. It was developed from the experiences of the industrial missioners who were devoted to evangelism of the factory workers and the urban poor of the 1960s and the 1970s in Korea.[1] Their effort to communicate the gospel message to the poor laborers, i.e., the minjung, who were living in great suffering and agony from the economic injustice and political oppressions, was not successful. Traditional interpretations of the gospel, or the "pre-packaged gospel" from the West, could not persuade the minjung, much less transform their lives.[2] The minjung could not see that the gospel message had any relevance to their daily lives filled with physical pains and emotional exasperation. The traditional presentation of the gospel and the other-worldly vision thereof could not properly address the torment, hopelessness, and anger in their lives. For this reason, the missioners began to reread the Bible from the perspective of the minjung and tried to find the meaning of the gospel that was relevant to the social and historical reality of the minjung.[3]

---

1. Yong-bock Kim, *Messiah and Minjung*, 3–5; Kwang-sun Suh, "Korean Theological Development," 38–41.
2. Yong-bock Kim, *Messiah and Minjung*, 4.
3. Ibid., 4–5.

REDEMPTION THAT LIBERATES

The Birth of Minjung Theology

It was during the early 1970s that the topics of the minjung and their suffering became a theological concern. The industrial mission groups held conferences where theologians were invited to engage in theological reflections on the missioners' experiences in the lives of the minjung and their effort to communicate the gospel message to them. Serious attempts were made by several theologians to interpret the gospel message from the perspective of the minjung, which resulted in the articulation of minjung theology during the second half of the 1970s.[4] Byung-mu Ahn and Nam-dong Suh published their first theological discussion of minjung in the same issue of *Christian Ideology* in April 1975 and, according to Jin-Ho Kim, this signaled the birth of minjung theology.[5] The year 1979 marked the epoch of the development of minjung theology when the Asian Theological Consultation was held in Seoul under the sponsorship of the Commission on Theological Concerns of the Christian Conference of Asia and the Korean National Council of Churches. This meeting served a significant venue for the minjung theology discussion of Korean theologians in dialog with other Asian theologians to elucidate and advance minjung theology.[6]

Minjung theology embraces a range of theological endeavors with different focuses and even disagreeing views on certain issues. There is a unifying theme in them, however, that brings those theological thoughts together under the name of minjung theology, and it is the centrality of the minjung in human salvation, which is commonly expressed as "minjung messianism." In what sense the minjung can be understood as the Messiah, however, has been controversial among minjung theologians; some take the statement "The minjung are Messiah" as meaning that the two are essentially identical while others take the statement as signifying that the minjung play a messianic role in salvation.[7] There is a clear agreement in minjung theology, however, that the minjung are not an object of charitable aid but the subject of the salvation history by their endurance of suffering from the injustice of the world that victimizes the minjung. This victimization of the

---

4. Kwang-sun Suh, "Korean Theological Development," 41.

5. Jin-Ho Kim, "Hermeneutics of Ahn," 19.

6. Kwang-sun Suh, "Korean Theological Development," 41–42.

7. As will be elaborated later in chapter 5, this is one of the major differences between Byung-mu Ahn and Nam-dong Suh.

minjung is regarded as their messianic sacrifice for the world.[8] The rest of the world, then, is saved by repentance and solidarity with the minjung.[9]

Definition of Minjung

The development of minjung theology can be understood in terms of the concept of the minjung. The question "Who is the minjung?" has been one of the central issues in minjung theology discussions. Minjung theology in the 1970s (the first-generation minjung theology) refused to define whom the minjung are. Kwang-sun Suh, for example, argues that defining the minjung in terms of the *proletariat* does not do justice to the reality of the minjung because the minjung are not limited to the laboring class in Marxist political economy.[10] Minjung is a dynamic concept, it is argued, that should be understood not only in terms of economic and political relationships but also from social, cultural, and historical perspectives. The first-generation minjung theologians commonly maintain that any attempt to define the minjung would inevitably objectify them and thus result in distorting the dynamic reality of the minjung. Nam-dong Suh, for example, observes that the definition of the minjung should be different from society to society, and from time to time, depending on the societal structure in which the minjung find themselves.[11] Instead of by scientific analysis, they argue, the minjung should be understood by their social biography characterized by the exploitation, discrimination, oppression, and alienation they suffer from due to their powerlessness.[12] For this reason, they reject the terms "citizens," "people," "folks," or "the masses" as improper translations for the minjung and insist on using the term *minjung* untranslated. Nevertheless, they maintain a basic characterization of the minjung as those who are economically deprived, politically oppressed, and socially alienated.

---

8. For example, see Ahn, *Discourse on Minjung Theology*, 32–33; Nam-dong Suh, *Study in Minjung Theology*, 180–81, 217. Ahn identifies the suffering and death of Jesus with the suffering and death of the minjung and argues that the minjung are the Lamb of God who takes away the sins of the world. Suh, on the other hand, contends on the basis of Jesus' parable of the Sheep and the Goats in Matt 25:31–46 that the minjung are the Messiah because the latter comes in the guise of the former.

9. For example, see Nam-dong Suh, *Study in Minjung Theology*, 181, 402.

10. Kwang-sun Suh, "Korean Theological Development," 42.

11. Nam-dong Suh, *Study in Minjung Theology*, 183.

12. For example, see Yong-bock Kim, *Messiah and Minjung*, 7–8.

Minjung theology in the 1980s (second-generation minjung theology) developed a distinctive understanding of the minjung by adopting Marxist social analysis and class theory. Won-don Kang, one of the representative thinkers of second-generation minjung theology, embraces the Marxist materialist worldview and tries to harmonize it with the Johannine theology of incarnation in an attempt to emphasize the primacy of practice over theory and to turn minjung theology into a movement.[13] For him, the Johannine statement that the Logos became flesh is a divine affirmation of the significance of the material world and life. Chang-rak Kim, another key thinker of second-generation minjung theology, argues that the minjung should be defined from the perspective of class contradiction.[14] For him and other second-generation minjung theologians, the proletariat (working) class, who is exploited by the bourgeoisie (capitalist) class, is the nucleus of the minjung. In contrast to first-generation minjung theologians, second-generation minjung theologians view not simply the military dictatorship but the capitalist class in collusion with imperial power as the oppressive ruling power and understand the minjung in terms of class struggle.[15]

Along with the political changes in the late 1980s and the early 1990s,[16] there has been another change in doing minjung theology. Third-generation minjung theologians since the 90s employ post-structuralism as an interpretive tool and include diverse movements in minjung theological reflections instead of focusing on a class struggle or labor liberation movement as a single grand discourse of minjung theology. Jin-Ho Kim, one of the most prominent thinkers of third-generation minjung theology, argues that in changed social and political situation minjung theology must be ready to engage in diverse transformation movements in local, national, and global levels, not only in class solidarity but also in solidarity with people of different social strata.[17] With respect to the understanding of the minjung, third-generation minjung theologians are no longer concerned with the question of who the Messiah is. They give attention to messianic events rather than to the identity of the Messiah and regard various liberation movements as messianic events. In this regard, they

13. Kang, *Theology of Matter*, 122–23.
14. Chang-rak Kim, "Meaning of Minjung," 129–30.
15. Jin-Ho Kim, "Minjung Theology," 28–29.
16. For example, the end of the military regimes in South Korea by the 1987 democratization movement and the end of the Cold War Era.
17. Jin-Ho Kim, "Minjung as the Subject of History," 46–47.

take not only the minjung but also citizens as the subject of the liberation movement of minjung theology.[18]

In addition to the generational distinction in the development of minjung theology, there have been two distinctive tendencies in doing minjung theology: the post-theology approach and the theological reconstruction approach.[19] While the former has been the mainstream, the latter continues raising voices. The post-theology approach seeks for an alternative community as an antithesis to the traditional church and proposes minjung theology as an alternative to traditional theology.[20] In contrast, the theological reconstruction approach recognizes the church as the proper field of minjung theology and seeks for harmony with traditional theology. With regard to the significant role of the minjung in salvation, this approach upholds it without necessarily rejecting the traditional christological proposition that Jesus is the Messiah in a unique way. Currently, minjung theology is still considered a theology in progress and minjung theologians in both approaches seek to affirm its contemporary relevance. While the theological debates are vital, the development of minjung theology cannot be adequately understood without considering the praxis it has inspired.

Solidarity with the Minjung

The industrial missioners' efforts in the 1960s and the 1970s to make the gospel message relevant to the minjung who had suffered social, economic, and political injustice led them to the solidarity with the minjung in their struggle for liberation. The gospel of Jesus, it was reasoned, concerns not only individual human souls but also their social lives in concrete situations and, therefore, sharing the gospel must be embodied in resisting social evils that suppress the human rights, dignity, and freedom of the minjung. During the tyrannical military regimes of the 1970s and the 1980s, laborers were exploited in the name of national economic development and, consequently, human rights and political freedom were repressed. Minjung theologians and the ministers influenced by minjung

---

18. In response to the changed social and political situation, Anselm Min even contends that the citizen, rather than the minjung, should be the subject of the liberation movement. Min, "From the Theology of Minjoong."

19. Choi, "Generational Approach," paras. 2–4.

20. Byung-mu Ahn, for example, suggested building "a life community" as an alternative to the traditional church. Jin-Ho Kim, "Hermeneutics of Ahn," 17.

theology in that period were devoted to the promotion of democracy and human rights, raising a prophetic voice against the unjust and oppressive military dictatorships. In those days, most churches and church leaders remained silent on the social and political injustice of that time while some of them even actively supported the unjust regimes. The Korean church in general seemed to give an uncritical endorsement to the oppressive dictatorships, and it was against this background that the minjung churches and theologians raised a prophetic voice. Several minjung theologians, including Nam-dong Suh and Byung-mu Ahn, were imprisoned and expelled from their professional posts, and many other participants in the minjung church movement were also persecuted.

The minjung church movement was a grassroots movement inspired by minjung theology. In an attempt not only to serve the minjung but also to identify with them in solidarity for their liberation, devoted pastors began to establish churches in the middle of slums and provide social services that were not otherwise accessible to them, such as labor-related counseling, day care services, after-school classes, night schools for GED, free weekend clinics, and libraries for poor neighbors. The 1980s witnessed a significant increase in the number of minjung churches. In 1988, the Coalition of the Minjung Church Movement in Korea was formed and there were more than 80 participating minjung churches. By 1992, the number of minjung churches grew to more than 150 churches that were actively involved in social ministries for the poor.[21] The year 1987 marked a turning point for the minjung church movement when the people of South Korea regained the right to vote in the presidential election (as a fruit of the long pro-democracy movement). Since then, the minjung church movement has been adjusting itself to the changing situation in response to challenging issues such as labor rights, globalization, neoliberalism, and environmental problems, as these issues bear direct impact on the lives of the minjung. Currently, while reduced in number and weakened in its influence, the minjung church seeks to establish its identity as a church open to various ministries that meet the needs of the minjung today. With this brief survey of the historical development of minjung theology, a consideration of its theological methodology is indispensable for understanding the essential characteristics of minjung theology.

---

21. Sang-si Jung, "New Prospect," 147.

Methodology of Minjung Theology

Theology from Below

There has been a way of characterizing a theology in terms of *theology from above* or *theology from below*.[22] Doing theology from above is to start from the Scriptures as the most authoritative divine revelation. One clear example is John Calvin, as Barth observes, "Without the biblical revelation that defines God the Redeemer Calvin sees no real knowledge of God the Creator."[23] Doing theology from below is to start from human experience and then to engage in theological reflections in the light of the Scriptures. James Cone provides a lucid example of this approach when he says, "To put it simply, Black Theology knows no authority more binding than the experience of oppression itself. This alone must be the ultimate authority in religious matters."[24] Calvinist theology is usually defined as a theology from above while liberation theology is generally characterized as a theology from below. In this regard, A. Wati Longchar characterizes minjung theology, along with other Third World contextual theologies, as a theology from below that is grounded in the experiences of poor and marginalized people.[25] This distinction, however, can run the risk of an oversimplification; there is no way to do theology purely from above or exclusively from below. Doing theology from above does not necessarily preclude human experience or reason as a legitimate source of theology. Doing theology from below also doesn't need to reject the Scriptures as an authoritative source. In fact, every theology utilizes these two ways of doing theology together in some way or another.[26]

22. For a recent example, see Olson, *Modern Theology*, 129.

23. Barth, *Theology of John Calvin*, 164.

24. Cone, *Black Theology*, 120.

25. Longchar, "Teaching Third World Contextual Theologies," 9. See also Ryoo, "Study of the Minjung Theological Spirituality," 81.

26. In this regard, Byung-mu Ahn rejects the so-called text/context dichotomy. The movement "from context to text," as expressed in such methodological statement as "Let the context interpret the text, not vice versa," is often considered one of the most significant hermeneutical principles of minjung theology in contrast to the traditional hermeneutical principle of "from text to context." Ahn, however, argues that text and context cannot be separated. For him, understanding of context is not possible without presupposing a perspective shaped by textual knowledge, while text cannot be interpreted in a vacuum without due consideration of context. The text/context dualism or subject/object dualism, according to him, is alien to Asian ways of thinking and thus cannot be a proper

These characterizations, therefore, should be understood as an "ideal type" in Max Weber's sense. As an ideal type, theology from above or theology from below is not meant to correspond to all aspects of a particular theology but to highlight the dominant theological approach that characterizes it. Both Calvinist theology and liberation theology, for example, take both the Scriptures and human experience as legitimate sources of doing theology in the sense that interpretation of one sheds light on the understanding of the other. In this regard, Max Stackhouse's reaffirmation of the four sources of doing theology is illuminating. He suggests that any cogent theology should be formulated on the classical ecumenical criteria of Scripture, tradition, reason, and experience. These so-called quadrilateral principles, he argues, should be utilized not in a way that each of them is invoked as a mutually exclusive source of authority, but in a way that "we need all four touchstones, each constantly refining and elaborating our understanding of the others."[27] Every theology, however, does not use the quadrilateral sources of the Scriptures, tradition, reason, and experience in the same way as others do.

Minjung theology, though it does not claim experience to be the sole foundation of doing theology or to have an exclusive authority over against other sources, nevertheless puts significant emphasis on the experience of the minjung. The suffering of the minjung, according to Namdong Suh, is an index of what God is doing in history, and Suh's statement that minjung theology studies the minjung rather than Jesus should be understood in this sense.[28] Minjung theology certainly employs other sources of doing theology such as the Scriptures, reason, and tradition. Yet, minjung theology has a distinctive way of utilizing the quadrilateral sources, especially the Scriptures and experience. The relationship of the Scriptures and experience in minjung theology is like that of *theoria* and *praxis* in liberation theology. *Praxis* in liberation theology is not just a mechanical application of *theoria*; rather, it confirms or corrects *theoria*, and the modified *theoria* in turn guides the *praxis* in a more constructive way. In a similar way, the experience of the minjung's suffering from injustice prompts rereading and reinterpretation of the Scriptures, and the Scriptures understood from the minjung perspective in turn reinforce

---

tool for minjung theology. See Ahn, *Discourse on Minjung Theology*, 65–70.

27. Stackhouse, *Public Theology*, 4.

28. Suh, *Study in Minjung Theology*, 47, 53.

the minjung movement of liberation.[29] Minjung theology, thus, does not discount the significance of the Scriptures in doing theology but puts priority on experience as the hermeneutical key. Only with these considerations taken into account can minjung theology be fairly called a theology from below in contrast to a theology from above. In relation to this, another important methodological principle of minjung theology is its use of Scripture and non-Christian traditions.

The Use of Scripture and Other Sources

The use of Scripture in minjung theology corresponds in some degree with James Gustafson's suggestions. He argues:

> Ultimately for Christian ethics, a biblically informed theology provides the bases for the final test of the validity of particular judgments: For Christians these judgments ought to be consistent, consonant, coherent with the themes that are generalized to be most pervasive or primary to the biblical witness.[30]

Gustafson, however, does not uphold the principle of *sola Scriptura* in this case. He does not consider the Scriptures the solely authoritative source for theologically informed judgments. Rather, he suggests "a dialectic between more intuitive moral judgments and both scriptural and nonscriptural principles and values."[31] For him, the task of the Christian community is to discern God's activities and demands for human beings in concrete social and historical situations and, in discerning this, Scripture alone is not sufficient but should be used in conjunction with other sources.[32]

In a similar vein, in his formulation of minjung theology Nam-dong Suh uses both Scripture and nonscriptural literature, and both Christian and non-Christian traditions, in discerning what God is doing in and through the minjung. He defines theology as a project of interpreting and reinterpreting the Scriptures with languages and ideas of the times.[33] Yet, he does not see the Scriptures as an absolute norm for doing theology but as "a point of reference" along with other valid reference points, such as his-

---

29. Yong-bock Kim, *Messiah and Minjung*, 4–5.
30. Gustafson, "Place of Scripture," 451.
31. Ibid.
32. Ibid., 452.
33. Suh, *Study in Minjung Theology*, 162.

tory, tradition, and experience.[34] He contrasts the "point of reference" with "revelation," defining the former as belonging to the historical category and the latter to the category of pure religion. For him, the task of minjung theology is to reflect on the mission of God (*Missio Dei*) in Korean history to promote human rights and to liberate the minjung.[35] The traditional religious category of revelation, according to him, does not provide an adequate tool for discerning the *Missio Dei* in Korea and hence he employs three reference points for his minjung theology: liberation events in Scripture, revolutionary ideas in church history, and Korean minjung tradition. After exploring these sources, Suh concludes that "in the Mission of God in Korea there is a confluence of the minjung tradition in Christianity and the Korean minjung tradition."[36] Kwang-sun Suh, too, contends that "the social biography (story) of the minjung" and "the Bible and Christian theology" interpreted from the minjung perspective are the two reference points for minjung theology, and the task of minjung theologians is "to interweave the Korean minjung story and the biblical story."[37]

The use of non-Christian sources in minjung theology is a corollary of the *Missio Dei* theology that minjung theology embraced. In this approach, God's salvific plan and activity are not limited to the revelation in Jesus. Minjung theology is intended to witness God's involvement in history and the work of the Holy Spirit both beyond biblical revelation and outside of the Jesus event.[38] Hence, minjung theologians utilize such Korean minjung traditions as grassroots cultures with themes of resistance to existing social order, popular religious beliefs in the radical change of the world, and revolutionary historical events and movements as warrantable sources of doing minjung theology.

With regard to the use of Scripture, minjung theologians maintain that the liberation of the minjung is the most fundamental theme of the biblical witness and the principal key to scriptural interpretation. There is nonetheless a slight difference among them concerning the interplay between Scripture and experience, or between text and context, to put it another way. For example, it is said that Byung-mu Ahn's way of doing minjung

---

34. Ibid., 184.
35. Nam-dong Suh, "Confluence," 239.
36. Nam-dong Suh, "Historical References," 177.
37. Kwang-sun Suh, "Korean Theological Development," 42.
38. Ahn, "Reply to the Theological Commission," 204; Nam-dong Suh, "Historical References," 177.

theology is from text to context while Nam-dong Suh's is from context to text. Ahn, however, rejects this general distinction as misleading. According to him, Suh does not simply begin his minjung theology from context or the minjung traditions but looks to context with his preunderstanding already shaped by Scripture.[39] In contrast, Ahn claims that while his minjung theology is solely grounded in Scripture and nothing else, there is no dualism of text and context in his thinking.[40] His interpretation of Scripture is nevertheless influenced by his own idea of minjung and controlled by his sociological perspective. Considering this, there is no fundamental difference between Ahn and Suh in their use of Scripture. In minjung theology, Scripture is not used as an exclusively authoritative source, nor is it treated as secondary to the minjung's experience. Rather, it is utilized in a dialectical way with the experience of the minjung because the minjung are regarded as having an epistemological advantage in understanding the divine salvific activity in and outside of Jesus.

Epistemological Advantage of Minjung

Minjung theology does not just espouse the idea of the divine preferential option for the poor minjung, but it also asserts the epistemological superiority of the minjung. It maintains that the minjung, because of their suffering from social, economic, and political injustice, are not only the object of divine mercy and preferential love, but they have "epistemological advantage" with which they can perceive the reality of the human condition more clearly.[41] James Cone, when he argues that black theology takes the experience of suffering as the ultimate criterion of theological reflection, does not mean that black theology puts priority on experience rather than on Christ. By this, he rather claims that "black people have come to know Christ precisely through oppression, because he has made himself synonymous with black oppression."[42]

In the same vein, in minjung theology the minjung know Jesus through their suffering from injustice and oppression and this puts them in a better place to understand the meaning of the suffering, death, and resurrection of Jesus more plainly. The rich and the powerful, in contrast, cannot understand

39. Ahn, *Discourse on Minjung Theology*, 68.
40. Ibid., 69.
41. Kyong-jae Kim, "Seed of Grain," 212.
42. Cone, *Black Theology*, 120.

Jesus' teaching properly. For instance, they cannot understand the meaning of the Lord's Prayer, in which the poor minjung are to ask for daily bread and divine forgiveness as they, the oppressed, forgive the oppressors. Nam-dong Suh thus argues that the rich and the powerful do not deserve to pray the Lord's Prayer until they repent of their social and political sins.[43] Further, in minjung theology Jesus showed favoritism toward the minjung, his mission was for the minjung, and Jesus himself was one of them. On this basis, minjung theologians regard it as self-evident that the minjung have the advantage in understanding the being and works of Jesus. Thus, it is generally maintained that minjung theology is not a theology *for* the minjung but a theology *of* the minjung, as it is grounded in their experience and directed by their perspective. In this sense, it is argued that the emphasis of minjung theology is not on doing theology as an objective scholarship but on clarifying and promoting the praxis of the minjung.[44]

Minjung theology involves methodologies different from the traditional ones and proposes many creative interpretations and ideas. This has provoked heated controversies and criticisms among both domestic and international theologians.

Criticisms of Minjung Theology

Criticisms of minjung theology can be classified into three categories: practical, theological, and exegetical. Practical criticism concerns itself with the relevance of the principal statements of minjung theology developed in the 1970s and the early 1980s to Korean society since 1987.

Practical Criticism

It is Kyung-suk Suh who triggered the controversy about the relevance of minjung theology in a changed society.[45] Once a fervent adherent of minjung theology and a dedicated social activist in the anti-dictatorship movement against the military regimes, Suh changed into a civil society activist after South Korea reestablished the direct election of the president in 1987, which was generally considered a restoration of electoral and

---

43. Nam-dong Suh, *Study in Minjung Theology*, 13, 402.
44. Ahn, *Discourse on Minjung Theology*, 72.
45. Kyung-suk Suh, "Crisis of Minjung Theology."

procedural democracy after the sixteen years of military dictatorship. He established the Citizens' Coalition for Economic Justice in 1989 and argued that changed times required a changed approach to the social transformation movement. According to him, middle-class citizens, instead of the minjung, are the central agent of social change as they have become the vast majority of the Korean population and their significance in social movements has increased since the so-called democratization process in the Korean society in the late 80s. For him, Korean society can no longer be characterized by military dictatorship or by conflicts between the haves and the have-nots.[46] Further, middle-class citizens cannot be easily categorized either as oppressors or as the oppressed, and according to Kyung-suk Suh they have the potential to work together to promote the common good of the society. For him, the framework of minjung theology is outdated and not adequate for the social transformation movement for changed times; thus he suggests the civil society movement as an alternative to the minjung church movement.[47]

Anselm K. Min presented a similar proposal.[48] Like Suh, he grounds his argument in the new situation of Korean society and questions the contemporary relevance of minjung theology. Since 1987, according to Min, Korean society has undergone three fundamental changes: democratization, bourgeoisification, and globalization. Due to democratization, he argues, a more civilized way of social communication and change is possible; the bourgeoisification of society has increased the influence as well as the number of middle-class citizens; and the globalization of society has brought about diverse issues as the topics of theological reflection. In consideration of these changes, Min concludes that the minjung are "no longer the bearers of history in Korea."[49] For him, citizens are a more realistic and efficient agent of social transformation in the contemporary Korean

---

46. For some people, the statement that "times have changed" is not a sufficient justification for criticizing the contemporary relevance of minjung theology. One may argue that Warren Buffett can be a defeater of such criticism because the American billionaire still believes that there is class struggle even in contemporary American society. He said to CNN in 2005, "It's class warfare; my class is winning, but they shouldn't be." Dobbs, "Buffett," para. 42. Again, in his interview with the *New York Times* in 2006 he argued, "There's class warfare, all right, but it's my class, the rich class, that's making war, and we're winning." Stein, "In Class Warfare," para. 6.

47. Kyung-suk Suh, "Crisis of Minjung Theology," 198.

48. Min, "From Theology of Minjoong."

49. Ibid., 23.

society, and hence he argues that minjung theology "must be sublated into the theology of the citizen."[50] While the criticism of the relevance of minjung theology inevitably involves theological criticism, a more serious theological criticism arises with regard to minjung messianism.

Theological Criticism

Minjung theology has developed a Christology that is radically different from the traditional statements. Byung-mu Ahn, for example, argues that it is mistaken to see Jesus as a person or to seek any significance in his person. For him, Jesus should be understood as an event of the collective experience of the minjung.[51] Ahn also argues that the Suffering Servant in the book of Isaiah, the Lamb of God in the Gospel of John, and the scriptural title of Messiah all refer to the minjung, and not exclusively to Jesus of Nazareth.[52] So-called minjung messianism has not only become one of the most fundamental propositions of minjung theology, but it also has been the major target of severe criticism.

For Reformed theologians, minjung theology has gone beyond the legitimate boundary of Christian theology because its primary concern is not God or Christ but humans and their advancement only in this life.[53] Eunsoo Kim, among others, thus argues that minjung theology, in its attempt to contextualize Christian theology in the Korean social and political situation, succumbed to unwarranted syncretism, humanization, and secularization.[54] According to Seyoon Kim, although minjung theology is claimed to have its basis on the historical Jesus, minjung theologians' portrayal of the historical Jesus, in fact, has no historical or biblical evidence; they just tend to use the term "Jesus' or "Crist" only as a symbol to support their own ideology.[55] They resort to minjung traditions in and outside of Scripture in order to, as they argue, interpret Jesus more properly. According to Kim, however, this shows that they failed to make a proper distinction between the particulars of God's salvific activity through the people of Israel that

---

50. Ibid., 20.
51. Ahn, *Discourse on Minjung Theology*, 26.
52. Ibid., 32–33, 93–98.
53. Eunsoo Kim, "Minjung Theology in Korea," 62.
54. Ibid.
55. Seyoon Kim, "Is 'Minjung Theology,'" 269–70.

climaxed in Jesus and the particulars of divine providence in promoting liberation and justice in human history.⁵⁶

It was not just some conservative theologians who voiced criticism of minjung theology; even some minjung theologians and those theologians who are sympathetic to minjung theology have raised questions concerning minjung messianism. Tae-soo Yim, one of the minjung theologians, argues that the minjung messianism proposed by Byung-mu Ahn is a stumbling block for the development of minjung theology.⁵⁷ In response to Ahn's statement that the minjung are the Lamb of God who carries away the sins of the world, Yim claims that only Jesus is the Lamb of God in the redemptive sense, who must be clearly distinguished from the minjung in this regard. Yim agrees that the minjung are carrying the sins of the world as they suffer from the injustice of the world. The sins that the Lamb of God carries away as mentioned in John 1:29, however, are not sins only in terms of political or economic injustice. He points out that *hamartia*, the Greek word for sin, primarily means in Scripture personal infringement in relationship to God. The sins of the world, then, must include both social sins in terms of political oppression and economic exploitation and personal sins in terms of ethical and religious infringements.⁵⁸ For that reason, the minjung are not qualified to carry away the sins of the world as a whole, nor can they be identified as the Messiah. Yim thus concludes that Jesus, not the minjung, is the Messiah.⁵⁹

Jose Bonino calls attention to the same problem in minjung messianism, which he calls "messianic confusion."⁶⁰ For him, it is one thing to say that "Jesus identified himself with '[the minjung]' or 'the poor'" and it is quite another to say that "the latter are 'identical' with Jesus Christ."⁶¹ This Latin American liberation theologian maintains that the dialectics of transcendence and incarnation in Jesus should be kept in order not to lose "the concrete historicity of Jesus the Christ."⁶² Similar criticism was raised by Jürgen Moltmann. For him, God is "with us" in Jesus in our suffering and, at the same time, God is "for us" in Jesus in our guilt.⁶³ To put it another

56. Ibid., 271.
57. Yim, "New Understanding," 77–78.
58. Ibid., 79.
59. Ibid., 80–81, 86.
60. Bonino, "Latin American Looks," 167.
61. Ibid.
62. Ibid.
63. Moltmann, *Jesus Christ*, 38; Moltmann, *Experiences in Theology*, 256.

way, Jesus is in solidarity with the minjung and, at the same time, he is the representation of the minjung as the Lamb of God in an inimitable way. These two statements, according to Moltmann, should not be confused, nor should one be taken as an alternative to the other. He recalls that he was shocked by Byung-mu Ahn saying that the minjung are the Suffering Servant of God in Isaiah 53 and the Lamb of God who bears the sins of the world.[64] For Moltmann, the unwilling endurance of suffering from social injustice by the minjung cannot be identified with the voluntary and vicarious suffering of Jesus. Minjung theology, according to him, has elevated the minjung to the status of the Messiah, but this is an unwarranted romanticization of the minjung by those who do not belong to them.[65] As the discussion above shows, the main theological criticism of minjung theology is focused on christological issues. Further engagement in theological criticism of minjung theology in general, however, is beyond the purpose and scope of our current study. Yet, any critical survey of minjung theology will be found incomplete without dealing with the exegetical issues, discussion of which, therefore, is in order now.

Exegetical Criticism

One of the most trenchant criticisms of minjung theology comes from Seyoon Kim, particularly in respect to its exegetical problems. The New Testament scholar understands that minjung theology is based on the interpretation of *ochlos* ("a crowd" in Greek) in the Gospel of Mark. According to minjung theologians, Mark uses the term *ochlos* as a socioeconomic term to refer to those who are poor, oppressed, and despised under the unjust social order. Minjung theologians see the *ochlos* as the minjung of Jesus' time and, according to their interpretation of Mark, Jesus accepted the *ochlos* (minjung) unconditionally and identified himself with them. While Pauline epistles and other Gospels, according to them, present distorted

---

64. Moltmann, *Experiences in Theology*, 258. In response to such criticism as Bonino's and Moltmann's, several contemporary minjung theologians want to point out the so-called subject/object dualism in such criticism and argue that the problem lies not so much in christological disagreement as in metaphysical difference. In this regard, attempts have been made to reinterpret minjung theology from the perspective of process theology. See Hiheon Kim, *Minjung and Process*; Kang-gil Jung, *Whitehead and Reconstruction of Minjung Theology*.

65. Moltmann, *Experiences in Theology*, 257. Further discussion of Moltmann's criticism will follow in chapter 5 in relation to Nam-dong Suh's minjung messianism.

and doctrinated description of Jesus, Mark provides the story of the real and historical Jesus. Kim raises serious questions about their exegesis of Mark and argues that their interpretation is guided by extrapolation and speculation rather than by the logics of sound exegesis.

First, according to Kim, it is "totally arbitrary" to suggest without any reasonable textual support from Scripture that the *ochlos* are socially, economically, and religiously alienated people.[66] He finds Byung-mu Ahn's definition of the *ochlos* (the minjung) to be too loose and self-contradictory as it includes the tax collectors into the category of minjung. Thus he observes, "Though [the tax collectors] may have been despised by the religious people, they were nonetheless powerful exploiters of the poor, enemies of the minjung, and targets of the closest approximation to a nationalist-liberationist minjung movement of the day—the zealots!"[67] For him, it is also problematic to regard, as minjung theologians do, Jesus as one of the minjung. Citing Martin Hegel's study, Kim maintains that Jesus was not a poor carpenter but a skilled worker (a *tekton* in Greek) who belonged to the middle class.[68]

Second, Kim questions minjung theologians' interpretation of the attitude of Jesus toward the *ochlos* (the minjung). Jesus, according to them, simply identified himself with the *ochlos* and accepted them unconditionally without attempting to judge, teach, enlighten, or exhort them. For them, calling the *ochlos* to repentance of their sins is a Lukan distortion of what Jesus really did to the minjung, which is, according to Mark, just calling them without demanding repentance. Kim, however, points out that even in Mark's Gospel Jesus always taught the *ochlos*, demanded them to repent their sins and believe in him, and admonished them for their lack of faith.[69] Even though Jesus showed partisan love toward the minjung, Jesus never accepted them without qualification; in fact, Mark included the saying of Jesus toward the *ochlos* in 3:35, which reads, "Whoever does the will of God is my brother and sister and mother,"[70] thus "pointedly distinguishing between those of the

---

66. Seyoon Kim, "Is 'Minjung Theology,'" 263.

67. Ibid., 264. To avoid this problem, Ahn distinguishes between rich and poor tax collectors. See Ahn, "Jesus and Minjung," 144–45. Kim takes this attempt of Ahn as an arbitrary interpretation "born of desperation."

68. Seyoon Kim, "Is 'Minjung Theology,'" 264.

69. Ibid., 265, 268.

70. Unless otherwise noted, all Scripture quotations are from the New Revised Standard Version.

ochlos who do the will of God and those who do not, and furthermore showing that Jesus identified himself only with the former."[71]

Third, Kim criticizes the inconsistency of minjung theologians in using the text of Mark's Gospel in support of their argument. Ahn, for example, takes the saying of Jesus in Mark 3:34, in which he identifies those gathering around him as his mother and brothers, as belonging to the original Gospel of Mark characterized by unconditional recognition of the *ochlos*. He totally ignores, however, the conditional clause in the immediately following verse that puts obedience to the will of God, rather than merely being the *ochlos*, as the criterion of his acceptance.[72] Kim is not persuaded that the Gospel of Mark is *ochlos*-centered whereas other Gospels distort the original message of Mark out of theological interest. He points out the "exegetical consensus" that Luke, rather than Mark, "shows the greatest concern for the poor and oppressed."[73] Mark, on the other hand, shows Jesus' affection as not limited to the poor minjung but also extended to rich and powerful people such as Jairus, the synagogue ruler, and tax collectors. For Kim, Mark is not different from other Gospels in presenting Jesus as the Messiah who through his teaching, vicarious death, and resurrection brings in the kingdom of God for all people regardless of class and race. Minjung theology, however, utilizes only part of Mark's Gospel in "a selective, arbitrary, tendentious, and self-contradictory" way.[74] Kim thus concludes that minjung theology has no support from Scripture because not only Mark's Gospel as a whole but even its few texts selected by minjung theologians also fail, if proper exegesis is employed, to provide a scriptural basis for it.[75]

In this chapter, we have discussed the historical development of minjung theology, its method, and its criticism from various perspectives. While the discussion is never meant to be exhaustive, for the purpose of our current study it will suffice to serve as a preliminary survey for the discussion of Nam-dong Suh's articulation of minjung theology. With this understanding, we now turn to a preliminary survey of the neo-Calvinist worldview that underlies Richard Mouw's political theology.

---

71. Seyoon Kim, "Is 'Minjung Theology,'" 268.
72. Ahn, "Jesus and Minjung," 141; Seyoon Kim, "Is 'Minjung Theology,'" 266.
73. Seyoon Kim, "Is 'Minjung Theology,'" 267.
74. Ibid., 268.
75. Ibid., 270–71.

3

A Preliminary Survey of the Neo-Calvinist Worldview

Theological Background of the Neo-Calvinist Worldview

RICHARD MOUW'S POLITICAL THEOLOGY is developed on his understanding of the neo-Calvinist worldview.[1] The neo-Calvinist worldview is a worldview formulated on the Reformed understanding of history as God's redemptive providence. An adequate analysis of his political theology then involves engaging first in the discussion of the neo-Calvinist worldview. In this chapter, we will discuss the theological background of the neo-Calvinist worldview, its principal ideas, its criticism from different perspectives, and the Korean Christian movement inspired by this worldview.

Definition of the Neo-Calvinist Worldview

The term *worldview* in our discussion refers to a basic belief system that functions as a fundamental perspective from which its subscriber understands the world.[2] The *world* here means everything, visible and invisible, about which it is possible to make a value judgment. A worldview can in

---

1. The neo-Calvinist worldview is also called the "Reformed world and life view," the "Reformed worldview," the "reformational worldview," or the "Kuyperian worldview." These terms all refer to the same idea and thus are used interchangeably in our study.

2. As a philosophical concept, worldview (*Weltanschauung* in German) was first used by Immanuel Kant in his work *Critique of Judgment*, published in 1790. For a historical survey of its concept and usages in various academic disciplines, see Naugle, *Worldview*, especially 55–67 for the history of the term.

this sense include even spiritual beings as objects of its consideration. It is this comprehensiveness of the concept of a worldview that attracted neo-Calvinist thinkers to translate their Reformed theological conviction as a worldview that is usually called the neo-Calvinist worldview.[3] With regard to the term "neo-Calvinist," Mouw argues that the prefix "neo-" does not denote any significant modification of the original ideas of Calvinism, while it does reflect a development of certain themes (by some Dutch Reformed theologians of the nineteenth and twentieth centuries) that were not consciously discussed in the early forms of Calvinist thought.[4] Thus, the neo-Calvinist worldview as a theoretical construct was distinctively shaped by Dutch neo-Calvinists such as Abraham Kuyper, Herman Bavinck, Herman Dooyeweerd, and D. H. T. Vollenhoven, while its theological influences can be traced back to Irenaeus, Augustine, Tyndale, and Calvin.[5] Of these thinkers, Calvin and Kuyper are most worth considering in our study as they have left the most pivotal influence in the formulation of the neo-Calvinist worldview. What follows is not a full study of Calvin or Kuyper, but an analysis of key themes that Mouw draws on.

John Calvin on Transformation of Culture and History

Calvin never used the word "worldview" or any equivalent term in his theology because the term as a theoretical concept had not been developed in his time. Yet, he is recognized as one of the most significant representatives of the Reformed worldview. This is due to his broad understanding of redemption in Christ. For Calvin, the redemption in Christ effects the restoration of the original order of all created things. Against Manichean dualism, he holds that the world is not divided into the two kingdoms, i.e., Satan's and God's kingdoms, but is one kingdom under God's sovereignty.[6]

---

3. In this regard, Naugle observes, "Conceiving of Christianity as a worldview has been one of the most significant developments in the recent history of the church." Naugle, *Worldview*, 4

4. Mouw, "Foreword," xi. According to Bob Goudzwaard, "'Neo-Calvinism' is an expression which was first used by Max Weber in his contributions to the sociology of religion. He used it to describe the revival of the social and political teachings of John Calvin which took place, especially in the Netherlands, during the last part of the nineteenth and the beginning of the twentieth centuries." Goudzwaard, "Christian Social Thought," 251.

5. Wolters, *Creation Regained*, 1.

6. Calvin, *Commentary on John*, 14:30. All quotations from Calvin's commentaries are from the AGES Digital Library *Comprehensive John Calvin Collection*.

According to him, though Satan is exercising his tyranny over the world, Christ by his redemptive death has begun to reclaim his kingdom. Commenting on John 12:31 ("Now is the judgment of this world; now the ruler of this world will be driven out."), Calvin agrees with those who translate the word "judgment" (*mishpat* in Hebrew" as denoting "reformation" rather than "condemnation," because the Hebrew word *mishpat* means "a well-ordered state."[7] On this basis, he understands the first half of the verse as meaning, "The world must be restored to a proper order," and argues that "(Christ's) death was the commencement of a well-regulated condition, and the *full* restoration of the world."[8] Under Satan's tyrannical dominion, according to him, sinful distortions and wickedness are found everywhere, but the death of Christ overturned Satan's dominion and began to bring back the world from satanic disorderliness to the original good order under the government of God.[9] For him, as the disorderliness of the creation under Satan's tyranny is all-encompassing, so is the restoration commenced in Christ. Satan deformed "all things," he maintains, but Christ reformed "all things" by his death.[10]

H. Richard Niebuhr is one of those who well recognized the transformationist character of Calvin's theology. In his now classic work, *Christ and Culture*, Niebuhr classifies Christian attitudes toward culture in five types and regards Calvin as a representative of the fifth type, "Christ the Transformer of Culture."[11] According to Niebuhr's presentation of the transformationist or conversionist type, the Christian moral vision does not replace the moral values of the world but restores them to the true order. Application of the gospel to the cultural life, then, is not thought to aim at establishing a new society but at transforming the currently existing society.[12] This transformative approach to culture, Niebuhr states, "is prominent in [Calvin's] thought and practice."[13] Niebuhr's classification of Calvin, however, cuts both ways; it illuminates the transformative nature

---

7. Ibid., 12:31
8. Ibid. (italics added).
9. ibid., 12:31; 16:11.
10. Ibid., 16:11. See also his *Commentary on Acts*, 3:21. Further discussion will follow later in this chapter where we deal with an interpretation of Calvin from the two kingdoms perspective.
11. His five types are: Christ against Culture, Christ of Culture, Christ above Culture, Christ and Culture in Paradox, and Christ the Transformer of Culture.
12. Niebuhr, *Christ and Culture*, liv.
13. Ibid., 217.

of Calvin's thought quite clearly in a comparative way with other Christian thinkers while it provides a limited understanding of the scope of redemption in Calvin's theology. This calls for more elaboration in order to achieve a coherent understanding of the relationship between transformation and redemption in Calvin.

Niebuhr's understanding of cultural transformation in his discussion of the conversionist type is motivated by the idea of universal redemption, which can hardly be reconciled with Calvin's understanding of redemption in Christ. In fact, Niebuhr is well aware of Calvin's dualistic understandings of human life as a "temporal and eternal existence" and its final destination as "an eternal heaven and an eternal hell." Niebuhr, however, seems to consider these an unessential "separatist and repressive note" accompanying the otherwise consistent transformative vision in Calvin's theology.[14] Without fully taking into account Calvin's eschatology and his teaching of the limited atonement, however, it would be impossible to adequately evaluate his understanding of the nature and scope of redemption in Christ. In this regard, Niebuhr's enlisting of Calvin as a representative of the transformationist type seems problematic.

In so far as the transformationist type is identified by Niebuhr's own definition based on universal redemption, Calvin does not fit neatly into that category and seems to call for a different, yet still transformation-driven, category for him. Of course, Niebuhr's typology, as Gustafson points out, must be understood in light of his ideal-typical method. This method, if properly applied, will help both the writer and the reader understand one type as one of many types classified in "disciplined disinterestedness" without using any value scale.[15] Therefore, the belonging of one specific thinker to an ideal type does not necessarily mean that the whole of that person's thought should completely correspond with the type. Ideal types, as Gustafson articulates, are "ideal constructs of idea along a clearly stated axis by which particular aspects of issues of literature are illumined."[16] Thus, an ideal type cannot serve as a comprehensive framework for understanding the whole ethical thought of a historical figure exemplifying that particular type. For this reason, Gustafson repeatedly calls for attention that the five types in Niebuhr's *Christ and Culture* must be recognized as ideal types in order to avoid mistaken criticism.

14. Ibid., 218.
15. Gustafson, "Preface," xxviii–xxix.
16. Gustafson, "Preface," xxx.

Nevertheless, one may still consider it problematic to put Calvin into the transformationist type of Niebuhr's own definition even as an ideal type. The "clearly stated axis" of the transformationist type in Niebuhr's typology is the transformation of culture based on the gospel of universal redemption.[17] Calvin's understanding of redemption, however, is significantly different from that of Niebuhr in terms of the goal and process of history; Calvin maintains radical discontinuity between history and eschaton whereas Niebuhr understands eschatology as immanentizing of the eschaton, i.e., consummation of cultural transformation within history.[18] In light of this, it is doubtful that any "particular aspects" of Calvin's understanding of redemption can be meaningfully "illumined" by the idea of transformation toward universal redemption. There can be no doubt that Calvin's ethic is transformative. However, one cannot properly evaluate Calvin's transformative ethic without recognizing what Niebuhr calls "a separatist and repressive note" accompanying the whole of Calvin's ethic. Though Niebuhr depicts it in a negative tone, the dualistic element in Calvin's ethic is not a setback from his more prominent vision of cultural transformation: it is not peripheral but essential to Calvin's understanding of redemption.

The transformationist type in Niebuhr's typological study shows a different concept of transformation from that of Calvin in terms of eschatology. The difference between dualistic eschatology and universalism makes one wonder if Calvin can be legitimately called a transformationist in the sense of Niebuhr's classification. There has been another way to interpret Calvin's view of cultural transformation in terms of redemption in Christ without subscribing to the idea of universal redemption or immanentized eschaton. Neo-Calvinism is a theological endeavor of some Dutch Calvinists of the nineteenth and twentieth centuries in seeking to do more justice to the all-inclusive nature of Calvin's understanding of redemption in Christ without compromising the essential elements of his theology. Abraham Kuyper, though not the sole contributor to this theoretical movement, is without question considered its most influential theorist who laid its foundation.

---

17. Niebuhr's universalist accent can be found throughout chapters 6–7 of *Christ and Culture*.

18. For Niebuhr's view, see Niebuhr, *Christ and Culture*, 195–96, 200–201, 204.

REDEMPTION THAT LIBERATES

Abraham Kuyper

While a faithful adherent to Calvinism, Abraham Kuyper is commonly known for bringing to full fruition one of the most significant features of Calvin's theology: the sovereignty of God over all aspects of reality. He is one of the rare thinkers whose ideas are consciously and consistently reflected in their careers. A journalist, theologian, politician, educator, and statesman, Kuyper is most well known as the founder of the Free University of Amsterdam in 1880 and as the prime minister of the Netherlands from 1901 to 1905. His efforts in such areas as education, culture, politics, and theology are motivated by his conviction that God is sovereign and Christ is the Lord over all dimensions of reality and human life. Thus he famously said in his inaugural address at the Free University, "There is not a square inch in the whole domain of our human existence over which Christ, who is Sovereign over all, does not cry: 'Mine!'"[19] This idea of an all-encompassing lordship of Christ certainly does not originate from Kuyper but is already existent in Calvin's thought, not to mention Paul or Augustine. Yet, Kuyper must be credited for consciously developing the idea and consistently applying it to the whole realm of human existence in conjunction with the all-inclusive character of Christ's redemption.[20] His view finds expression especially in his utilization of the idea of worldview.

For Kuyper, traditional apologetics is not an adequate tool for defending Christian faith against competing secular thoughts or religions. It is not simply two conflicting doctrines or ideas, according to him, but two "life systems" or "life and world views" that are fighting against one another in "mortal combat."[21] For him, modernism was the greatest threat to Christian faith in his times, and the Christian apologetic approach was found totally ineffectual. Patchy apologetic defense, according to him, is like trying "to adjust a crooked window-frame, while . . . the building itself is tottering on its foundation."[22] In modernism, he argues, "the vast energy of an all-embracing *life-system* assails us, then also it must be understood

---

19. Kuyper, "Sphere Sovereignty," 488.

20. Kuyper's development of Calvin's thought in this respect led him even to the point of some disagreements with the Reformer especially on the issues of Christian life in the public squire. This eventually resulted in the label of "neo-Calvinism" for the thoughts of Kuyper and his followers. Mouw, *Abraham Kuyper*, 80.

21. Kuyper, *Lectures on Calvinism*, 11.

22. Ibid., 135.

that we have to take our stand in a life-system of equally comprehensive and far-reaching power."[23]

A worldview, according to Kuyper, is an "all-embracing system of principles" that determines one's fundamental understanding of the human relationship to God, to human beings, and to the world.[24] Emphasizing the significance of a worldview and the urgency of holding a coherent Christian worldview to confront secularism, he asserts:

> As truly as every plant has a root, so truly does a principle hide under every manifestation of life. These principles are interconnected, and have their common root in a fundamental principle; and from the latter is developed logically and systematically the whole complex of ruling ideas and conceptions that go to make up our life and world-view. With such a coherent world and life-view, firmly resting on its principle and self-consistent in its splendid structure, Modernism now confronts Christianity; and against this deadly danger, ye, Christians, cannot successfully defend your sanctuary, but by placing, in opposition to all this, *a life- and world-view of your own, founded as firmly on the base of your own principle, wrought out with the same clearness and glittering in an equally logical consistency.*[25]

For Kuyper, Calvinism as broadly conceived provides the most effective form of Christian worldview as it concerns not simply dogmatic, confessional, or denominational interpretation of Christian faith but the entire range of human life including ethics, thoughts, cultures, politics, economics, and so on. According to him, what is distinctive in the Calvinist worldview is the cosmic, all-embracing nature of God's creation, humanity's fall, and the redemption in Christ.[26] Everything created is created according to divine ordinances and maintained by it. Humanity's fall has brought disturbance in the ordinances of God in creation, and redemption in Christ is not meant to add something new to the creational ordinances or to change them but to restore them by removing the disturbances and bringing cre-

23. Ibid., 11.
24. Ibid., 19.
25. Ibid., 189–90 (italics original).
26. Kuyper and most neo-Calvinist thinkers present the outline of the Christian worldview from philosophical and systematic theological reflections. Lamenting the lack of the biblical exegetical study on the Christian worldview, Richard Mouw provides a biblical study on the issue. See Mouw, *When the Kings Come*. Albert Wolters also offers a solid biblical as well as philosophical study on the Christian worldview. See his above-cited work, *Creation Regained*.

ation back to the accordance with the original ordinances of God. Thus, he neatly puts, "Christ has swept away the dust with which [humanity]'s sinful limitations had covered up this world-order, and had made it glitter again in its original brilliancy."[27] In this regard, Naugle aptly observes that what characterizes Kuyper's conception of Calvinist Christian worldview is "the idea that God's redemptive 'grace restores nature'; that is, the salvation achieved by Jesus Christ is cosmic in scope and entails the renewal of everything in creation to its original divine purpose."[28]

Like Niebuhr, Kuyper finds in Calvin a theological justification for Christian engagement in cultural transformation. Unlike Niebuhr, however, Kuyper sees the dualistic understanding of the human race and its final destination in Calvin's thoughts not as an unessential "separatist and repressive note"[29] but as a crucial aspect of his theology. In his discussion of the spiritual renewal through redemption in Christ, Calvin makes a clear distinction between those who belong to the new creation in Christ and those who do not and describes this division as "an antithesis between Adam and Christ."[30] Following Calvin, Kuyper elaborates further on the theme of the *antithesis* and argues that this antithesis is manifest in all human social, cultural, and intellectual activities. "[T]he fact that there are two kinds of *people* [redeemed and unredeemed]," he insists, "occasions of necessity the fact of two kinds of human life and *consciousness* of life, and of two kinds of *science*."[31]

Kuyper not only picked up the idea of the antithesis between the redeemed and the unredeemed from Calvin, but he also developed the concept of *common grace* in Calvin's thoughts. The antithesis, while it is real in principle, is not always clearly recognizable in reality because of the common grace of God that is operative in human life.[32] Calvin recognizes the moral, intellectual, and artistic capability and even excellence in fallen humanity and ascribes it to God's general grace as distinguished from the saving grace in Christ. Even the mind of the unredeemed, according to him, is still endowed with God's gifts of goodness and truth, and the Spirit

27. Ibid., 71.
28. Naugle, *Worldview*, 22.
29. Niebuhr, *Christ and Culture*, 218.
30. Calvin, *Institutes*, II.iii.6.
31. Kuyper, *Principles of Sacred Theology*, 154 (italics original); quoted in Mouw, *Abraham Kuyper*, 61 n. 5. By the term *science* Kuyper refers to human intellectual activities in a broad sense rather than natural or social sciences specifically.
32. Mouw, *Abraham Kuyper*, 67.

of God should be acknowledged as the genuine source of everything that is good and true. Therefore, Calvin insists, "we shall neither reject the truth itself, nor despise it wherever it shall appear, unless we wish to dishonor the Spirit of God."[33] Kuyper develops the discussion of common grace further and argues that common grace impacts both interior and exterior aspects of human existence. For him, not only the orderliness of human life by general morality and virtue but also the advancement and enrichment of human life by science, art, and technology should be attributed to the common grace of God.[34] Further, according to Kuyper, common grace is the mysterious working of God's grace that makes cultural development possible and creation progress even under the fallen condition of humanity.[35] In this regard, common grace and redemption work together; common grace enables cultural development while redemption in Christ effects cultural transformation.

The exclusiveness of the antithesis and the inclusiveness of common grace may seem contradictory to each other. Kuyper, however, does not endorse one idea at the cost of the other but integrates them in his understanding of the Calvinist worldview. The central theme of God's redemptive grace restoring creation recognizes the continuity between creation and redemption. In this thinking, the idea of common grace reinforces the continuity because common grace points to the remaining of the goodness of creation; grace does not replace the fallen creation with totally new things but reclaims it. For Kuyper, however, this does not necessarily mean universal redemption. He maintains the antithesis that supposes a radical discontinuity between the redeemed and the unredeemed. According to him, Christ's redemption, while encompassing all domains of human life and relationships, is differentiated from common grace and is rather associated with saving grace for the elect. This shows the fundamental difference between Kuyper and Niebuhr in understanding the nature and scope of redemption in Calvin's thoughts.

While Kuyper laid the foundation of the neo-Calvinist worldview, its more articulate expressions came from worldview commentators during the 1980s, which witnessed a renewed interest in the worldview discussion.[36]

---

33. Calvin, *Institutes*, II.ii.15.
34. Kuyper, "Common Grace," 181.
35. Mouw, *Abraham Kuyper*, 68.
36. Several important works were published in this period to stimulate the worldview discussion. To list a few but not limited to: Wolters, *Creation Regained*; Holmes, *Contours of a World View*; Marshall et al. ,eds., *Stained Glass*; Walsh and Middleton, *Transforming*

Explicitly and implicitly, most commentators of the Christian worldview are influenced by Kuyper and among those commentators Albert Wolters is considered one of the most prominent writers who presents a clear and coherent exposition of the neo-Calvinist worldview directly inspired by Kuyper. With this survey of the theological development of the neo-Calvinist worldview, we now turn to the consideration of its pivotal ideas by reviewing Wolters' discussion.

Creation–Fall–Redemption–Consummation

The Worldview and the Scriptures

In contrast to the methodological priority of context over text in minjung theology, the neo-Calvinist worldview is based on the reformational principle of *Sola Scriptura*. In this approach, Scripture is regarded as "the *principium cognoscendi*, the principle of knowing or cognitive foundation of theology," according to which the priority of Scripture is upheld over tradition, reason, and experience in discerning all matters of beliefs and morals.[37] Thus Albert Wolters, a leading commentator of this worldview, calls it a reformational worldview in his seminal work, which, along with the works of several other thinkers during the same period, triggered a renaissance in the Christian worldview discussions in the 1980s. He explicates the reformational worldview as based on the biblical teachings of "the depth and scope of sin and redemption."[38] Foundational in this worldview is the scheme of *creation–fall–redemption–consummation*,[39] which is

---

Vision; Mouw, *When the Kings Come Marching In*; Frey et al., *All of Life Redeemed*; Hart, *Understanding Our World*; Hoffecker and Smith, eds., *Building a Christian Worldview*; Hart et al., eds., *Rationality in the Calvinian Tradition*.

37. "Sola Scriptura," in Muller, *Dictionary*, 284. Regarding the fact that Scripture is held as authoritative and normative in Protestant ethics, James Gustafson observes, "Just as the theory of a natural moral law set the boundaries within which debates took place in Catholic moral theology, so it is not unfair to claim that the debates within Protestant ethics took place within the boundaries of Scripture." Gustafson, *Protestant and Roman Catholic Ethics*, 21.

38. Wolters, *Creation Regained*, 1.

39. Wolters' book *Creation Regained* provides discussions of *creation*, *fall*, and *redemption* in three separate chapters for each topic but has no dedicated chapter for a discussion of *consummation*. This by no means implies that he precludes the vision of eschatological consummation from the reformational worldview. In fact, the final consummation is implicit in all his discussion of the worldview. See, for example, Wolters, *Creation Regained*, 70; Wolters, "Dutch Neo-Calvinism," 122.

understood as pivotal in the biblical metanarrative and as crucial in interpreting human history, life, and world. The essential insight of this worldview is *grace restoring nature*, which means the redemption in Christ is the restoration of the original good creation that has been perverted by sin. What distinguishes the neo-Calvinist worldview from other worldviews, including the worldviews of different Christian theological traditions, is its totalizing perspective on reality based on the biblical narrative conceived of as God's redemptive history. Wolters offers a very illuminating exposition of this worldview in terms of its all-encompassing character. The following summary of his exposition, while serving as a sketch of the central motifs of the neo-Calvinist worldview and by no means being a full systematic account of any of these motifs, will shed further light on the clear understanding of the neo-Calvinist worldview for our current study.

Creation: According to the reformational worldview, the totality of the physical world and the structures of human life is created and governed by the creational order. The creational order, or the creational law, refers to the Creator's sovereign will and design in constituting and upholding the totality of created reality. It refers not just to the law of nature, to which the physical world is subject, but also to the normativity that governs all aspects of human life, including societal and personal relationships. Every field of human affairs is so normed throughout by the law of creation that "everywhere we discover limits and proprieties, standards and criteria."[40] All societal structures, authorities, and institutions have certain constant features of their own as created nature that distinguish them from others. The fact that there are right and wrong ways of doing things that go beyond cultural relativity shows the existence of the creational law. In short, everything is creational and thus subject to the created order of God. Creation, however, is not meant to be a finished project but is embedded with potentials for growth, an unfolding of creation. For this reason, the Creator made humans in his image and gave them a mandate to develop the world he created. It is then humanity's responsibility to serve the Creator's purpose in every sphere of creation by taking part in the ongoing creational work of God. In this regard, eschatological consummation is viewed as more than what a perfect restoration of the original creation can bring about. Creation in its original state, according to the biblical

---

40. Wolters, *Creation Regained*, 22.

account, was "wholly and unambiguously *good*."[41] It is humanity's sin that perverts the originally good creation.

Fall: In the reformational worldview, all evil and perversity in the world result from the fall in which humanity refuses to live according to the good ordinances of God's creation. All of creation is under the deadly influence of humanity's sin; no created thing is in principle able to escape the corrosive effects of the fall.[42] Though sinful distortion affects all of creation, it cannot negate the creation. No matter how closely creation and sin are intertwined in human experiences, sin cannot replace creation, but rather its existence is like a parasite that attaches itself to creation. It exists only as a distortion of the good and cannot abolish the enduring goodness of creation, which refers to the faithfulness of God in upholding the created order despite humanity's fall.[43]

Redemption: Sin, no matter how extensively it permeates into the created reality, can never abolish any part of the originally good creation. Instead of abandoning some worse part of the fallen creation and saving other better part of it, God chose to regain all of it. As creation and fall are cosmic in their scope, so is redemption in Christ in the sense that it restores everything that is fallen. "This restoration," Wolters holds, "affects the *whole* of creational life and not merely some limited area within it."[44] Almost all of the basic words describing salvation in Scripture, such as "redemption," "reconciliation," "renewal," "regeneration," and "restoration," imply a return to an originally good state or situation. Thus, redemption of the creation in Christ means the "return to the goodness of the originally unscathed cre-

---

41. Ibid., 41.

42. This is what the notion of *total depravity* in Calvinist theology means. See Calvin, *Institutes,* II.i.9; Beach and Niebuhr, eds., *Christian Ethics,* 271.

43. Wolters, *Creation Regained,* 47–48. Here we can see an Augustinian influence on the formulation of the neo-Calvinist worldview. For Augustine, evil has no substance but is merely the absence of good. See Augustine, *Confessions,* VII.12, 18. Every sin, according to him, is misuse or distortion of originally good creation; nature, therefore, though tainted by sin, is good in itself. Thus Augustine maintains, ". . . evil cannot exist without good, because the natures in which evil exists, in so far as they are natures, are good." Augustine, *City of God,* XIV.11. For him, nature is not to be negated altogether, but to be restored to its original state, as he puts, ". . . evil is removed, not by removing any nature, or part of a nature, which had been introduced by the evil, but by healing and correcting that which had been vitiated and depraved." Ibid.

44. Wolters, *Creation Regained,* 57.

ation and not merely the addition of something supracreational."[45] In other words, God refused to abandon the fallen creation altogether, but decided to reclaim it. Redemption, therefore, is "the recovery of creational goodness through the annulment of sin and the effort toward the progressive removal of its effects everywhere."[46]

In the reformational worldview, the scope of the originally good creation, humanity's fall, and redemption in Christ is the totality of created reality and this holistic perspective keeps its subscribers from falling into the unnecessary dualism of the sacred and the secular in human life.

Consummation: The reformational worldview upholds that redemption in Christ reaches all areas of human life and that there is no single part of human social or personal life that is not under Christ's lordship. Despite some criticism,[47] this does not necessarily lead to cultural triumphalism or historical optimism because, in the reformational worldview, the redemption already begun in history is balanced with eschatological consummation that is to come at the end of history. Redemption in Christ, on the one hand, is something that has already begun to affect all created reality, and it is something that can be experienced here and now. Its completion, on the other hand, is something that must await the end of history. Using Oscar Cullmann's analogy of D-Day and V-Day, redemption initiated in the death and resurrection of Jesus, like D-Day, assures the final and complete victory, but the consummation as V-Day has yet to come, and the battle cannot be ceased until the day of final victory.[48] This "already but not yet" character of redemption in Christ in the reformational worldview makes it impossible to uncritically endorse both triumphalist optimism toward cultural transformation and other-worldly and pessimistic retreat from cultural transformation. There is no room for a dualism in the reformational worldview

---

45. Ibid. In the same vein, Wolters observes that "salvation is *re-creation*," by which he means that "grace does not destroy or supplement, but rather *restores* nature." Wolters, "Dutch Neo-Calvinism," 122.

46. Wolters, *Creation Regained*, 69. In this sense, neo-Calvinist philosopher Nicholas Wolterstorff argues that it is a Christian's responsibility to commit oneself to the reform of the fallen structures of one's society and, according to him, this is not additional but essential to Christian faith and spirituality. Wolterstorff, *Until Justice and Peace*, 3.

47. David VanDrunen, for example, criticizes the neo-Calvinist worldview as triumphalist and argues that it falsely views the redemption in Christ as including political and cultural transformations. For him, redemption involves only the spiritual kingdom of Christ. VanDrunen, *Natural Law*, 78, 253, 259.

48. Wolters, *Creation Regained*, 70.

that categorizes the creation into two realms, good and bad, or sacred and secular, applying redemption in Christ only to a limited area. At the same time, a continued tension is recognized and maintained between history and eschaton because redemption already begun is not to be completed in history but awaits the eschatological consummation.

In summary, the reformational or neo-Calvinist worldview provides a holistic perspective on reality with the cosmic interpretation of creation, fall, redemption, and consummation without allowing the idea of universal redemption or historical optimism. In addition, the practicability of the worldview should be also noted. Christian worldview is not just a matter of knowledge but also of practice. Christian worldview, as Naugle succinctly puts it, "*implies the objective existence of the trinitarian God whose essential character establishes the moral order of the universe and whose word, wisdom, and law define and govern all aspects of created existence.*"[49] In this sense, Mullin rightly observes that the Christian worldview involves "deep ontological, epistemological, and ethical commitments."[50] This is even more true for the neo-Calvinist worldview because its proponents present it as an all-embracing perspective on the totality of reality for the restoration of the created moral order. To borrow Karl Marx's well-known phrase from *Theses on Feuerbach*,[51] the neo-Calvinist worldview is not just concerned with interpreting the world but with changing it. In this sense, Albert Wolters insists that the neo-Calvinist worldview is similar to Marxism in terms of its "claim to comprehensiveness and immediate applicability."[52] With this understanding at hand, we now proceed to consider its criticism directed on several points, especially on the scope of redemption.

Criticisms of the Neo-Calvinist Worldview

As discussed above, it is clear that the neo-Calvinist worldview embraces a vision of cultural transformation as it is anchored in the notion of redemption in Christ that encompasses all areas of human life. While the transformative nature of the worldview is admittedly influenced by Calvin,

---

49. Naugle, *Worldview*, 260 (italics original).

50. Mullin, "Difficulties Surrounding," 3.

51. In his eleventh thesis on Feuerbach, Marx famously remarked, "The philosophers have only interpreted the world, in various ways; the point is to change it." Marx, *Karl Marx*, 23.

52. Wolters, "Dutch Neo-Calvinism," 117.

objections have been raised even within the Calvinist circle against viewing Calvin as a transformationist.

The Two Kingdoms Perspective

David VanDrunen, one of the leading polemics against transformationism, argues that the shared interpretation among many Reformed theologians of Calvin as a cultural transformationist is misled.[53] "The differences between Calvin and his neo-Calvinist followers today," he claims, ". . . are often striking, yet largely unobserved."[54] While assuming the influence of Niebuhr's typological study on those Reformed advocates of the transformationist approach to culture who claim Calvin as a representative of their vision, VanDrunen points out the complete lack of reference to Calvin's writings in Niebuhr's *Christ and Culture*.[55] From this he seems to suggest that Niebuhr's interpretation of Calvin as a transformationist does not have any textual support from Calvin's own writings.

Critical of the transformationist interpretation of Calvin, VanDrunen finds triumphalistic optimism in such interpretation and contends that Christian social engagement, though upheld by Calvin, has nothing to do with Christ's redemption in Calvin's theology. He rather interprets Calvin's social ethic from a perspective of the two kingdoms doctrine and argues that Calvin "divided the various spheres of life into two, identifying the church with the kingdom of Christ and the various other spheres of cultural activity with the civil kingdom."[56] Putting Calvin in opposition to his transformationist interpreters, VanDrunen believes that "Calvin makes a categorical distinction between the church and the rest of life and identifies the kingdom of Christ and the promise of redemption only with the former."[57] It is Calvin's conviction, according to him, that the idea of redemption has nothing to do with cultural activity and therefore Calvin "disallows the gospel, in which the message of redemption lies, from being applied to the civil kingdom."[58] It should come as no surprise, then, that VanDrunen calls into question Niebuhr's classification of Calvin and

53. VanDrunen, "Two Kingdoms."
54. VanDrunen, *Natural Law*, 4.
55. VanDrunen, "Two Kingdoms," 248 n. 2.
56. Ibid., 253.
57. Ibid.
58. Ibid., 259.

Luther into different categories from each other.⁵⁹ He seems to argue that, in Niebuhr's typology, Calvin should be placed along with Luther in the two kingdoms category, i.e., the "Christ and Culture in Paradox" type, rather than in the transformationist type.

VanDrunen contends that Calvin's view of natural law is interrelated with his two kingdoms doctrine in a way that leads to the dualistic understanding of the Christian life in society. While affirming the continuity of Calvin's natural law understanding with the medieval natural law tradition, he argues that Calvin applies different roles of natural law to the civil and spiritual kingdoms: "Calvin ascribed surprisingly positive use for natural law (in the form of various cultural achievements) in his discussions of life in the civil kingdom and consistently negative use for it (in the form of leaving all people inexcusable for their sin) in his discussions of life in the spiritual kingdom."⁶⁰ According to VanDrunen, implications of the different roles of natural law are clear for Calvin: natural law is a useful divine instrument for maintaining peace and justice in the civil kingdom, where God rules but without effecting redemption, while it is not so useful in the spiritual kingdom, where God is carrying out redemptive activity through the Word and the Spirit.⁶¹ In conclusion, VanDrunen argues that Calvin's ethic is based on the dualist categories of the spiritual and civil kingdoms. According to him, Calvin maintained throughout his theological career that God's redemptive activity takes place not in all areas of creation but only in the spiritual kingdom of Christ. Admitting that Calvin does have a positive view of cultural engagement for the purpose of making a difference in common social life, VanDrunen nevertheless asserts that for Calvin "it was not redemption in Christ that justified such engagement."⁶² Consequently, he describes Calvin as a political conservative rather than a transformer. "Calvin believed," he avers, "that the civil kingdom was to remain the civil kingdom, and he was modest in his hopes of changing it."⁶³

VanDrunen's argument is polemical enough to stimulate heated debates on one of the most essential ideas of the neo-Calvinist theological vision: cultural transformation as part of Christ's redemption. From the perspective of the Kuyperian Calvinists, however, his challenge is not

---

59. VanDrunen, *Natural Law*, 69 n.4.
60. Ibid., 110.
61. Ibid., 113.
62. VanDrunen, "Two Kingdoms," 266.
63. Ibid., 264.

convincing enough to rebut the common interpretation of Calvin and Calvinism as transformationist. Timothy Palmer is one of those who refute VanDrunen's claim as grounded on an incorrect reading of Calvin. While not denying the fact that Calvin does have his own version of the two kingdoms doctrine, Palmer argues that "the lordship of God and the kingship of Christ are more determinative in Calvin's theology."[64] For him, the cultural transformationism of Calvin and Calvinism stems from Calvin's understanding of the universal rule of Christ as not excluding the earthly kingdom. Another scholar in Kuyperian tradition, Jason Lief, repudiates VanDrunen's criticism on the basis of Calvin's anthropology.[65] According to Lief, Calvin does not have a Platonic dualism of body and soul but holds a holistic understanding of the human person as an integrated unity of body and soul. From this perspective, the spiritual and the temporal as the two spheres of human life are inseparably linked together, and as a result Calvin sees redemption in Christ as affecting not only the spiritual but also the temporal life. In Calvin, Lief concludes, the kingdom of God is not to be reduced, as VanDrunen suggests, to the spiritual kingdom but consists of both the spiritual and the temporal realms, which are renewed by the redemption in Christ.[66]

VanDrunen criticizes the transformationist interpretation of Calvin, which is the central idea of the neo-Calvinist worldview, as misleading and incorrect. In response to this, those scholars with the neo-Calvinist background assert that VanDrunen's interpretation misses the essential thrust of Calvin's theology in exaggerating the two kingdoms doctrine, which, according to them, should be distinguished from Luther's idea.[67] While a detailed discussion of Calvin's theology is beyond the scope of this study, a brief observation of his understanding of redemption in Christ will show how the neo-Calvinist worldview is consistently grounded on Calvin's own thought.

---

64. Palmer, "Calvin the Transformationist," 33.
65. Lief, "Is Neo-Calvinism Calvinism?," 2–4.
66. Ibid., 8.
67. For example, see Kloosterman, "Response"; McIlhenny, *Kingdom Apart*; James Smith, "Reforming Public Theology."

Calvin's Idea of the Two Kingdoms and the Scope of Redemption

Neither Niebuhr's formulation of the transformationist type in his taxonomy nor the two kingdoms perspective do justice to Calvin's understanding of redemption in Christ. Calvin does use the two kingdoms language, especially when he discusses Christian freedom and respective authorities of the ecclesiastical and the civil governments.[68] Notwithstanding the perceptible similarities of the two kingdoms or two governments language between Calvin and Luther, however, there are clear differences between them with respect to the relationship of the spiritual kingdom to the civil kingdom.

According to Luther, God has ordained two different orders in the world with distinct purposes: the spiritual government or kingdom (*Das geistliche Reich*) for producing piety among true believers and the secular government or kingdom (*Das weltliche Reich*) for maintaining external peace and justice among the whole human race, believers and non-believers alike. Luther insists that "these two kingdoms must be sharply distinguished, and both be permitted to remain," while "neither is sufficient in the world without the other."[69] Calvin makes a similar distinction between the spiritual kingdom and the civil kingdom, and there is no difference between Luther and Calvin in terms of their understanding of the divine origin and the positive roles of the secular or civil kingdom. Luther's view, however, focuses primarily on the proper function of the civil kingdom. Regarding the life in the civil kingdom, he pays more attention to the goodness of the created orders and institutions than to their distortions in the fallen world. Thus, quoting 1 Timohty 4:4, which reads, "Every creature of God is good, and nothing is to be rejected by the believing and those who know the truth," Luther affirms the social and political orders as equally good providences of God as material necessities.[70]

---

68. Calvin, *Institutes*, III.xix.14–16; IV.xx.1, 3; and IV.xx.1.

69. Luther, *Martin Luther*, 371. It should be noted that these two kingdoms are both divinely ordained kingdoms. While they must be clearly separated, the two kingdoms are complementary to each other and both are in the service of God's purpose. On the other hand, there is another dualism of two kingdoms in Luther: the kingdom of God and the kingdom of the world. The former consists of those who are true believers in Christ and the latter of those who are not. Both are spiritual kingdoms in nature and categorically opposed to each other. These two kinds of the two kingdoms must not be confused. Ibid., 203, 368.

70. Ibid., 378.

While Luther primarily upholds the positive roles and goodness of the civil kingdom as constituted by divine providence, Calvin, in contrast, focuses more on the consequences of the fall permeated into all areas of the civil kingdom. With regard to the impact of the fall on the human person, Calvin famously states that "the whole [human being] is overwhelmed—as by a deluge—from head to foot, so that no part is immune from sin and all that proceeds from him is to be imputed to sin."[71] In this notion of total depravity Calvin does not suggest that all that is human is so completely ruined by sin that nothing good can be found in the human being. What he calls to attention in this rhetorical expression is not the degree but the *extent* of the influence of sin: sin has touched the entire sphere of human life and society. What Calvin intends to argue with his idea of total depravity is that humanity's fall into sin affects the *whole* human person in the will, intellect, affection, and the *entire* range of human interactions.[72] In the fallen world, according to him, not only human souls but also all human relationships, social orders, and institutions are under the corrupting influence of the fall. In fact, all of creation participates in the fall, and the civil kingdom is not an exception.

For Calvin, therefore, the redemptive work of Christ is applied not only to human souls but also to all of created reality, which is under the sinful distortion of the fall. The redemptive activity of Christ, according to him, is to bring the fallen creation back to its original state of good order. Thus, he maintains that "Christ restores to order those things which formerly were torn and decayed" and he calls this "a true restoration, by which *all things* are reformed."[73] He continues to write, "Satan, so long as he retains the government, perplexes and disturbs *all things*, so that there is an unseemly and disgraceful confusion in the works of God; but when he is stripped of his tyranny by Christ, then the world is restored, and good order is seen to reign."[74] Further, commenting on Acts 3:21, Calvin spells out the "already but not yet" character of the redemption. "As touching the force and cause," he contends, "Christ hath *already* restored all things by his

---

71. Calvin, *Institutes*, II.i.9.

72. In this regard, H. Richard Niebuhr takes Calvin's notion of total depravity as meaning that "the total human beings—in reason, will, religion, politics, etc.—were infected with the corruption." Beach and Niebuhr, eds., *Christian Ethics*, 271.

73. Calvin, *Commentary on John*, 16:11 (italics added). Commenting on John 12:31, Calvin also says that the death of Jesus was "the commencement of . . . the full restoration of the world."

74. Ibid., 16:11 (italics added).

death; but the effect doth *not yet* fully appear; because that restoring is yet in the course."[75]

In light of Calvin's view of the redemption in Christ as the restoration of all things, cultural transformation in Christ is not merely a good work to improve human and social conditions; it rather is part of Christ's work to redeem all that is distorted and corrupted by sin. For this reason, Calvin is clearly distinguished not only from the "Christ of Culture" liberalism that simply equates social progress with redemption, but also from Luther's two kingdom dualism that keeps the civil kingdom from the effect of redemption in Christ.

What distinguishes Calvin from Luther in their two kingdoms thinking is that Calvin has a more realistic understanding of the impact of sin on all areas of human life, which then leads to the broader understanding of the scope of redemption in Christ. In contrast, Luther's version of the two kingdoms is a static parallelism of the two kingdoms, which may give one a false impression of unwarranted dualism of church and state that promotes an uncritical support of the status quo. Though Luther recognizes that God rules not only over the spiritual kingdom but also over the secular kingdom, it would be unreasonable to suppose that God exercises his kingship over the civil kingdom without intending to redeem what is under Satan's dominion or without transforming what is distorted by sin. For this reason, Calvin seems to have a more consistent understanding of the two kingdoms doctrine based on Christ's redemption of all that was created but fallen.

The difference between Calvin and Luther in their understanding of the two kingdoms is also evident with regard to the nature of the law that rules over the kingdoms. For Luther, two different kinds of laws rule over the two different kingdoms, respectively: the law of Christ over the spiritual kingdom and the natural law over the secular kingdom.[76] While affirming the existence and the positive role of natural law, Luther clearly distinguishes it from the law of Christ. Calvin, in contrast, maintains a strong continuity between natural law and the moral teachings of Jesus.[77] He never conceives of natural law as a rudimentary law only for justice and orderly life in the civil kingdom with the law of Christ as a higher law applicable only to those in the spiritual kingdom of Christ. Instead, he understands them in terms of grace restoring nature: the general knowledge of the natural law is limited,

---

75. Calvin, *Commentary on Acts*, 3:21 (italics added).
76. Luther, *Martin Luther*, 380–82.
77. Calvin, *Institutes*, I.vi.1; II.viii.1, 7.

confused, and distorted due to the noetic effect of sin, and the moral teachings of Jesus are given to restore the true knowledge of the natural law.[78] For Calvin, God does not rule over the two kingdoms with two fundamentally different moral standards. There is only one law of God, according to him, that rules over all domains of human life. While the comprehension and practice of natural law in the civil kingdom are limited under the influence of sin, Calvin holds that the restored natural law should be normative not only in the spiritual kingdom but also in the civil kingdom: in the spiritual kingdom through spiritual transformation and in the civil kingdom through cultural transformation.[79]

As seen above, Calvin has a broader understanding of redemption in Christ than Luther does and understands the scope of redemption as including both spiritual renewal and cultural transformation. According to this observation, then, the anti-transformationist interpretation of Calvin by such polemics as VanDrunen and their criticism of the neo-Calvinist worldview cannot be reasonably maintained. There are yet several critical concerns raised within the neo-Calvinist circle that deserve our attention here.

Criticism from Within

One of the most frequent and substantial criticisms of the transformationist vision of the neo-Calvinist worldview is that it fosters unwarranted triumphalism in public activities. It is clear in the Calvinist thought that Christ's kingdom is not of this world. A cultural transformationist vision, however, may give a false impression that Christian social and political engagement can achieve a fundamental transformation here and now. Richard Mouw points out this triumphalist tendency in many of the Calvinist political

---

78. For Calvin and other Reformed thinkers, the existence of the natural law is never to be denied while its knowability is seriously limited due to the noetic effect of sin. Ontology of natural law, therefore, must be distinguished from its epistemology. As Oliver O'Donovan rightly points out, Karl Barth's vehement rejection of natural law is due to his failure in making such a distinction. O'Donovan writes, "In his pursuit of an uncompromised theological epistemology Barth allowed himself to repudiate certain aspects of the doctrine of creation (such as 'ordinances') which ought never to have fallen under suspicion." O'Donovan, *Resurrection and Moral Order*, 86–87.

79. According to Calvin, the moral law is not only used to condemn the wicked but also to guide human beings in their social and political life by providing them with a right moral standard. He writes, "[The moral law] is the true and eternal rule of righteousness, prescribed for [humans] of all nations and times, who wish to conform their lives to God's will." Calvin, *Institutes*, IV.xx.15.

endeavors, admitting that they have been "Constantinian."[80] While dismissing as overstatement John Yoder's contention that "Jesus' resistance to the third temptation in the wilderness [i.e., a refusal to use political power] was in effect a refusal to become a 'Calvinist,'" Mouw nevertheless admits that some Calvinists have been too optimistic in their understanding of what Christian political activities can bring about.[81] For him, the triumphalist approach to cultural transformation is misguided. Instead, he suggests a dialectic of hopefully *awaiting* the coming of transformation and actively *seeking* it with cultural and political engagement.[82]

Another danger observed in the neo-Calvinist worldview is its tendency toward intellectualism. The neo-Calvinist worldview, focused on creation order and its restoration, involves an intelligible explanation of the created normativity and its distortion in the present life. However, it tends to inspire less commitment to the transformation of the unjust social order. Effective in providing a coherent vision of far-reaching and radical transformation of the distorted order of creation, the neo-Calvinist worldview has not been so effective in inspiring its subscribers toward sympathization and solidarity with those who are suffering under the fallen order. In principle, it concerns both interpretation and change of the world. In practice, however, it is overridden with intellectualism and tends to focus more on a satisfactory description of the world with less transforming commitment. In this regard, Carroll Hart responds to Wolters's presentation of the neo-Calvinist worldview with the following rhetorical questions:

> Are we interested in enforcing law and order, or in transforming our culture so that it shows forth the love and justice of Yahweh? And let me ask this: Whose interest is the notion of creation order serving? The interests of a conservative established majority, or the interests of shalom in which those who were far may be brought near?[83]

In a similar vein, Wolterstorff detects a legalistic tone in the formulation of the neo-Calvinist worldview in terms of the restoration of the

---

80. Mouw, *Politics and the Biblical Drama*, 99.

81. Ibid.

82. Mouw, *When the Kings Come*, 75. In order to avoid triumphalism in Christian political activities, Mouw also suggests the prophetic dialectic of pessimism and optimism as a balanced approach to cultural transformation. See Mouw, *Politics and the Biblical Drama*, 121–24.

83. Hart, "Doctrine of Creation." 60.

creational order.[84] For him, creation cannot be reduced to legality. Focused more on the moral and rational order of creation, neo-Calvinist thought, according to him, is less concerned with *rights* embedded in creatures. The fallenness of the world, he contends, should not be understood only in terms of the moral disorderliness of human life but also of the brokenness of human life under various sufferings.

Well aware of the perils of intellectualism and legalism in the neo-Calvinist worldview, Mouw expresses his unease about the notion of "having a worldview." Instead of just grasping a worldview as a static idea, therefore, he suggests *"engaging in worldviewing,"* by which he means actively allowing the biblical perspective of redemption not only to shape one's way of thinking but also to guide one's behavior.[85]

The neo-Calvinist worldview has been understood as a movement due to its transformationist orientation.[86] Criticism of its intellectualist tendency, then, is not an objection to the worldview itself but rather an attempt to recover and reinforce its transformative character. In this regard, when the neo-Calvinist worldview was introduced to Korean Christians, it was not accidental that it inspired both theological renewal and a social transformation movement.

Christian Worldview Movement in Korea

It was the early 1980s that the neo-Calvinist worldview began to stimulate theological discussions and small group studies among Korean Christians. Under the military dictatorship of that time, young Korean Christians in the evangelical and Reformed tradition were struggling to find a biblical vision of social transformation that is doctrinally evangelical and sociopolitically responsible. Until then, it seemed to them that only two extreme positions were available in the Korean churches with regard to the Christian social engagement. If not giving blind support to the government, the majority of the churches were keeping silent on social and political injustice. On the other hand, a small number of minjung theologians and the advocates of the minjung church movement with liberal theological

---

84. Wolterstorff, "Points of Unease," 64–65.

85. Mouw, *Abraham Kuyper*, 93 (italics original).

86. Wolters regards neo-Calvinism as "a movement which combined spiritual and theological renewal with fresh beginnings on a broadly cultural front: political, social, economic, educational and academic." Wolters, "Dutch Neo-Calvinism," 118.

persuasion were resisting the oppressive dictatorial regime. Neither the social indifference of the conservative churches nor the anti-government resistance of the theologically liberal minjung church movement, however, was a convincing option for the socially awakened evangelical Christians. To them, both positions seemed inadequate; most of the Korean churches of that time ignored the biblical call for promoting justice and human rights, while the minjung church movement appeared to run the risk of losing Christian distinctiveness.

The Korean student movement against the military dictatorship of the early 1980s adopted Marxism as a scientific tool both for interpreting social and historical reality and for drawing a vision of changing society. There were evangelical Christian students who were seeking to find a way of social engagement that was consistent with their evangelical faith. It was at this juncture that the Christian worldview discussions of the Dutch and North American neo-Calvinists were introduced to them. The neo-Calvinist worldview was fervently received by the young evangelical Christians, and it served as a "scientific" tool to understand world and history from a Christian perspective. Those who felt stuck between the conservative, dualistic Christianity and the Marxist materialist worldview found a new, compelling vision of social transformation in it.

The Christian worldview influenced the Korean churches in two ways. First, it was a fresh challenge to the dualistic thinking and attitude that were dominant among most Korean Christians. The central theme of the all-encompassing nature of creation, fall, and redemption in the worldview provided a coherent alternative to the dualism of the sacred and the secular, or the spiritual and the worldly. In this regard, attempts have been made by Christian scholars of various academic disciplines to engage in their studies from the vantage point of the Christian worldview.[87] This worldview also gave an eye-opening experience to those who were not convinced by the dualism of church and society and were looking for a theological ground of evangelical social engagement. They eagerly studied the worldview and tried to disseminate it to the wider audience of the Korean churches through group studies, lectures, seminars, and publications. Those study groups that contributed to the introduction of the Christian worldview into the Korean churches developed into Christian

---

87. Their endeavors are reflected in the scholarly discussions stimulated by the publication of *The Journal of Integrative Studies* by the Society of Integrative Studies since 1988.

worldview research associations such as the Christian University Fellow Laborers Association (later, Disciples with Evangelical Worldview) and the Korean Association of Christian Studies.[88]

The other way the Christian worldview influenced the Korean churches was to motivate evangelical Christians into a social transformation movement. They were encouraged by the fact that there was a way to actively join the transformation movement of that time without subscribing to Marxist ideology or losing their Christian distinctiveness but still maintaining their evangelical convictions. After the establishment of the Christian Research Association for Cultural Study in 1986, the evangelical students influenced by the Christian worldview began to actively take part in transformation activities. They formed base communities with the urban poor and provided nursery and tutoring services for the children of working poor families. To help poor laborers they also established several night schools and offered vocational classes as well as classes for the Korean GED test. The Young Evangelicals Coalition and the Christian Young People and Student Association, established in 1987 and 1989, respectively, were also inspired by the Christian worldview and committed to the promotion of social, economic, and political justice in Korean society.[89] Study of the Christian worldview among young evangelical Christians led to active social engagement, though on a limited scale. For this reason, this phenomenon was called the "Christian worldview movement."

There were, however, disagreements among the advocates of the Christian worldview movement about what kinds of concrete strategies and methods of praxis would be employed. While the Christian worldview provided a cogent evangelical vision of social transformation, it was not a method of social analysis. Some in the Christian worldview movement, therefore, contended to make use of the Marxist methodology for the purpose of analyzing economic and political realities of Korean society. They wanted more active involvement in social transformation activities. Others opposed adopting Marxism even as a tool for social analysis and wanted to distance themselves from deeper social engagement for fear of losing Christian distinctiveness.[90] This chasm in part caused the decline of the Christian worldview movement since the early 1990s, and recently one of the young evangelical leaders contended that this model of evangelical

88. Hun-soo Kim, "Retrospective Essay," 191–92.
89. Ibid., 194–96.
90. Ibid., 196.

movement is now out of date.⁹¹ Though the praxis inspired by the Christian worldview had limited influence on society as a whole, its influence on the Korean churches cannot be underestimated. The Christian worldview movement opened the door to Christian social and cultural engagement from the perspective of an evangelical vision of social transformation. In fact, it can be comparable to the minjung church movement of the same period. We will visit this point again in a later chapter.

With this theological and historical survey of the neo-Calvinist worldview along with that of minjung theology in the previous chapter, we now turn to the comparative discussion of Nam-dong Suh's articulation of minjung theology and Richard Mouw's neo-Calvinist political theology. Our comparative discussion is grounded on the *both/and* way of thinking that Suh and Mouw share in their theologizing. In order to facilitate the comparison, therefore, we need to first define *both/and* thinking.

---

91. Jung-hoon Jung, "Korean Evangelicalism," para. 24.

4

The *Both/And* Way of Thinking

ONE OF THE MOST pivotal aspects that characterize both Suh's and Mouw's theological reflections is their *both/and* thinking, which contrasts with *either/or* thinking. According to Jung Young Lee, a Korean American theologian who attempts to understand the divine relationship in the Trinity with the yin-yang symbol, yin-yang symbolism is East Asian cosmology, which inspires the *both/and* way of thinking.[1] In this symbolism originated from ancient Chinese philosophy, everything in the universe and life is described by the interplay of yin and yang. Everything has its opposite, like light and darkness, and expanding and contracting, and those opposite forces are symbolized in terms of yin and yang. Yin (陰) literally means the shady side of a hill and yang (陽) means the sunny side of a hill. The two symbols designate the bipolarity in nature and life; yin signifies the moon, night, cold, downward movement, quiescence, contracting, death, and so forth, while yang signifies the sun, day, hot, upward movement, activeness, expanding, life, and so forth. More importantly, the earth represents yin, and the heaven yang. The fundamental duality of yin and yang is a cosmic and life principle by which everything can be categorized into the two contrary forces. According to this classical Chinese worldview, everything that exists operates and changes by the dynamic interaction between yin and yang.

The two opposite forces, however, do not conflict but in fact complement each other. Yin-yang symbolism is not a principle of static, unchangeable existence but of the dynamics of interrelatedness.[2] Something is defined as yin or yang by the proportion of yin or yang it has over the

1. Jung Young Lee, *Trinity in Asian Perspective*, 24–34; *Marginality*, 64–70. For an application of this approach to Christian living, see Nathan and Kim, *Both-And*.

2. In this regard, Lee argues that, in order to grasp the meaning of yin and yang, "we must alter the basis of our thinking from an ontological to a changeological assumption." Jung Young Lee, *Trinity in Asian Perspective*, 27.

other, and everything is described by the interaction between yin and yang within it. For example, day is yang not because it has no darkness at all but because it has more light than darkness. Yin and yang, therefore, cannot be separated from each other and cannot exist without each other. In yin-yang symbolism, yin and yang do not eliminate but embrace each other for harmonious interrelationship, in which one accompanies the other for a perfect unity. Lee calls this "complementary dualism" in contrast to "conflicting dualism."[3] In conflicting dualism, one polarity fights against the other and wins by removing it, and this corresponds with an *either/or* way of thinking. In complementary dualism, in contrast, the two polarities do not try to eliminate the other but maintain a harmonious balance because the opposite is also an integral part of the whole. This kind of dualism represents a *both/and* way of thinking.

The *both/and* way of thinking is a balanced and integrating approach to different, and even opposing, views whereas *either/or* thinking is a polarizing and exclusivist approach. According to Lee, the *either/or* way of thinking separates the opposites to contrast the differences while the *both/and* way of thinking allows the opposites not only to stand together but also to complement each other.[4] For him, the former is typical of the Western analytic approach to reality, whereas the latter is characteristic of the Eastern harmonious way of thinking.[5] Lee, however, does not simply promote *both/and* thinking over *either/or* thinking. Taking *both/and* thinking exclusively in rejection to *either/or* thinking, according to him, is already employing the *either/or* way of thinking.[6] In a truly inclusive *both/and* thinking, *either/or* thinking must have its proper place, and the two modes of thinking should be utilized in accordance with the nature of a subject matter. In discussing a theological matter, therefore, Lee contends that *both/and* thinking should be employed because the holistic and harmonizing way of thinking is more appropriate in dealing with the ultimate reality.[7] Wilfred Smith, admitting that the predominant way of thinking among the Western intellectuals is *either/or*, contends that a theological thinking must utilize

---

3. Ibid., 31.
4. Ibid., 33. See also Jung Young Lee, *Marginality*, 69.
5. Jung Young Lee, *Trinity in Asian Perspective*, 54.
6. Ibid., 33.
7. Ibid., 34.

the *both/and* approach. He writes, "In all ultimate matters, truth lies not in an either-or, but in a both-and."[8]

One of the most prominent advocates of *both/and* thinking in theological inquiry is John Stott. Admittedly one of the most influential thinkers of evangelical Christianity in the twentieth century, he warns against the polarizing tendency of both evangelical and progressive Christians. Polarization, according to him, is to uphold one polar area of truth while rejecting the opposite polar area of truth. "If we could straddle both poles simultaneously," he says, "we would exhibit a healthy biblical balance."[9] He cannot agree more with Charles Simeon, who wrote, "The truth is not in the middle, and not in one extreme, but in both extremes."[10] Theologically speaking, Stott believes that a balanced approach is open to both conservative and radical interpretations of the gospel. For him, when Martin Luther King Jr. said, "Religion deals with both heaven and earth," he clearly showed the *both/and* approach.[11] W. A. Visser't Hooft, the former WCC general secretary, showed another fitting example of this approach when he made the following statement during the Fourth Assembly of the World Council of Churches at Uppsala in 1968:

> I believe that with regard to the great tension between the vertical interpretation of the Gospel as essentially concerned with God's saving action in the life of individuals and the horizontal interpretation of it as mainly concerned with human relationships in the world, we must get out of that rather primitive oscillating movement of going from one extreme to the other.[12]

Stott warns against the danger of a polarizing tendency in theological thinking, according to which one side of truth is eagerly maintained with the other side of truth totally rejected. For him, the *both/and* way of thinking is a more viable approach to the complexity of theological truth than \ *either/or* thinking.[13] As our discussion in the following chapters shows, Suh and Mouw consistently employ the balanced *both/and* approach in their theological reflections in contrast to the *either/or* approach of Ahn and VanDrunen, and this is the most significant factor that contributes to the theological affinity between them.

8. Wilfred Smith, *Faith of Other Men*, 72; quoted in Jung Young Lee, *Trinity in Asian Perspective*, 33–34 n. 22, 23.

9. Stott, *Balanced Christianity*, 10.

10. Carus, ed., *Memoirs*, 600; quoted in Stott, *Balanced Christianity*, 11 n. 1.

11. King, *My Life*, 127; quoted in Stott, *Balanced Christianity*, 51 n. 3.

12. Stott, *Balanced Christianity*, 53–54.

13. Ibid., 55.

5

Anthropological Comparison: What Is the Human Problem?

Nam-dong Suh's Understanding of the Human Problem

A CHRISTIAN THEOLOGY IS AN attempt to answer questions arising from the fundamental problems of human life, and its answer is expected to be reasonably grounded in the Christian account of the ultimate. This chapter compares what Nam-dong Suh and Richard Mouw regard as the most fundamental human problem that triggers their theological reflections. Nam-dong Suh contends that the oppression and exploitation of the ruling power against the minjung is the root of the human problem. He defines the minjung not as the proletariat in the Marxist socioeconomic analysis, but as anyone who is alienated and oppressed by the unjust social order.[1] Approvingly citing the minjung poetChi-ha Kim, he agrees that, while the minjung were partners of the covenant with God in creation and the active subject of history appointed by God, they were alienated and oppressed by the dominating power.[2] Suh maintains that the power in fact originated from the minjung, but, once institutionalized, it usurped its master's seat and tyrannized them. According to him, therefore, salvation in history means taking the power back to its proper place, thereby

---

1. Nam-dong Suh, *Study in Minjung Theology*, 177.

2. Nam-dong Suh, "Historical References," 155–56. Following Chi-ha Kim, Suh claims that the divine mandate in Gen 1:28 that reads, "Be fruitful and multiply, and fill the earth and subdue it; and have dominion over the fish of the sea and over the birds of the air and over every living thing that moves upon the earth" was directed toward the minjung and not toward the dominators.

restoring divine justice.[3] In this line of thinking, the injustice of the ruling power is the root of humanity's sin, and the oppressed minjung, who are easily relegated to the category of sinners by the power, are rather innocent victims.[4] Suh, therefore, argues that the minjung are not those who sin, but "those who are sinned against."[5]

Sin and Han

Suh calls for a reconsideration of sin because sin, according to him, has been dogmatized to control the minjung by the ruling power. He contends that understanding sin only in terms of a personal and religious concept without its sociological analysis can result in distorting the original intents of the Scriptures.[6] Considering sin from a sociological perspective, he argues that sin is often conveniently used by the ruling power as a label for the powerless and the defiant. In this sense, the minjung who are labeled as sinners are not the ones who actually commit sins but the ones who are falsely condemned by the unjust order of society, which only serves the interest of the ruling power. It is for this reason, according to Suh, that the Markan descriptions of the minjung are not negative or judgmental, nor does Jesus in Mark demand repentance from the minjung.[7] This is contrasted by the fact that Jesus harshly criticized the ruling class, including the priests, scribes, Pharisees, and Sadducees. Suh takes the position that while sin is a term used by the ruling class, *Han* is the term used by the minjung. For this reason, he maintains that the problem of *Han* should receive more serious theological attention than that of sin.[8]

Han, as Suh describes it, is "an accumulation of suppressed and condensed experiences of oppression" in the hearts of the minjung.[9] It usually expresses itself in resentment toward unjustly inflicted sufferings or unwilling resignation to one's fate. When mobilized, it can serve as an intensive drive for

---

3. Ibid., 156.

4. It is not clear whether the dichotomy between the oppressors and the oppressed is a valid analysis of the complex dynamics of human social relationships. More discussion will be given later in this chapter.

5. Nam-dong Suh, "Envisagement of *Han*," 344.

6. Ibid.

7. Ibid., 343.

8. Ibid., 344.

9. Nam-dong Suh, "Toward a Theology of *Han*," 64.

resistance and, therefore, it is also called the "emotional core of anti-regime action."[10] *Han*, however, can serve as a destructive power of revenge, and thus Suh suggests that it should be overcome through *Dan*.[11]

Dan is a Korean word derived from the Chinese word *duan* (斷), which means an act of severing. The destructive *Han* that grows out of hatred toward oppressors and seeks for revenge is usually met with another oppression, which in turn causes another *Han* to grow. *Dan*, according to Suh, is to sever the chain of this vicious circle of *Han* by giving up revenge and seeking instead God's justice.[12] For him, this is what distinguishes minjung theology from a type of socialism, on the one hand, that resorts to violent revolution for social transformation and from a form of Western theology, on the other hand, that serves as an ideology for the ruling class by focusing on the sin of the minjung rather than their *Han*.[13] Quoting Chi-ha Kim sympathetically, Suh contends that the sublimation of *Han* from a destructive power of resentment and revenge to a constructive spiritual power is only possible through "religious commitment" and "internal and spiritual transformation."[14] This is where he finds the way the Christian church can serve the minjung for their liberation from *Han*. So he invokes Kim again: "The church ought to be the comforter to resolve the *Han* of the minjung and to cut the vicious circle of violence and to change it into a progressive movement."[15] It is the oppressed minjung, not the oppressors, according to Suh, who have the initiative to break the vicious circle of hostility and, based on this, he develops his minjung messianism.[16]

In his discussion of minjung theology, Suh gives greater emphasis to the problem of *Han*, but this does not mean that he totally rejects the problem of sin in relation to God.[17] Here we can detect his *both/and*

---

10. Ibid.

11. Ibid., 64–65.

12. Ibid. Suh closely follows Chi-ha Kim and heavily quotes from his works in understanding *Han* and *Dan*.

13. Nam-dong Suh, "Confluence," 273.

14. Nam-dong Suh, "Toward a Theology of *Han*," 65.

15. Ibid.

16. We will discuss Suh's minjung messianism in detail in the following chapter reserved for a christological comparison between Suh and Mouw.

17. Suh admits that his minjung theology is not intended to deal with all theological concerns equally. Nam-dong Suh, "Confluence," 272. He gives greater emphasis to social and political implications of the Christian message and, in this sense, he has a "preferential option" for authentic practice (*orthopraxis*) rather than authentic belief (*orthodox*).

way of theologizing. When he compares the traditional interpretation of Jesus with what he calls the pneumatological historical interpretation of him in minjung theology, Suh does not consider the two perspectives as conflicting. He not only advocates the pneumatological interpretation of Jesus, according to which we are called to imitate Jesus and replicate what he did to resolve the minjung's *Han*, but he also affirms the traditional interpretation, according to which it is believed that "Jesus of Nazareth has redeemed me from sin."[18] This shows that his discussion of the problem of *Han* is not in exclusion of the problem of sin.[19] He does not avoid using the language of sin and its redemption in Christ. He would definitely reject the language of sin, however, if it conveyed only a biased meaning in terms of personal and religious infringement for the interest of the ruling power while obscuring their social and political injustice.

Suh devotes serious attention to the injustice of the ruling power and contends that it causes the minjung's long-suffered *Han* and is the root problem of humanity. His understanding of the fundamental human problem, however, is not limited to the exploitative power relationship between the ruling class and the minjung. While criticizing Constantinian Christianity, in which the message of the kingdom of God is depoliticized and reduced only to spiritual concerns, Suh still recognizes that the kingdom of God is more than what a social and political revolution can bring about in history.[20] For him, the human problem lies not just in the social and political alienation of the minjung but also in the human spiritual alienation from God. In his discussion of Thomas Müntzer, whom he regards as a pioneer of the theology of the minjung, Suh agrees with him that spiritual renewal and social reform must go together without one taking priority

---

While it is without question that *orthopraxis* and *orthodox* are inseparably connected to each other, Suh intentionally gives weightier attention to what has been long overlooked. In a similar vein, he sees salvation as liberation from social, economic, and political injustice and oppression. He contrasts his pneumatological historical interpretation of the Scriptures with an existential interpretation and makes it clear that he is more concerned with a "political interpretation" than a personal and religious one. Nam-dong Suh, *Study in Minjung Theology*, 166.

18. Nam-dong Suh, "Historical References," 177. His method of pneumatological historical interpretation will be further discussed in the following chapter of this study.

19. Kyong-jae Kim observes that Suh does not neglect sin in personal and spiritual dimensions. See Kyong-jae Kim, "Seed of Grain," 211. See also Nam-dong Suh, *Study in Minjung Theology*, 202.

20. Nam-dong Suh, "Historical References," 162.

over the other.[21] This inclusive and holistic view of the root of the human problem by Suh can be more clearly understood when it is compared with the view of Byung-mu Ahn, another leading minjung theologian.

Byung-mu Ahn's Understanding of the Fundamental Human Problem

Ahn maintains that what lies at the root of the human problem is the violation of *kong*. *Kong* is a Korean word that means "public" or "shared." If something is *kong*, as he explains, it "cannot be privatized," and it is "for all and yet belongs to no one."[22] According to Ahn, everything in the world is *kong* because God is the creator and true owner of everything. He opposes any view that regards the private ownership of property and the political order as intrinsic to the divine order of creation.[23] The problem of humanity, then, is understood to have begun when privatization against *kong* began to take place. For him, privatization of wealth and power is the fundamental deviation from God's design for human life and the root cause of the human problem. Repentance, in this line of his thinking, is "a concrete act that restores *kong*."[24]

The essential sin of humanity, according to Ahn, is the privatization and monopolization of wealth and power that victimize the minjung. He does not propose that the minjung are sinless, but his concept of sin is limited to its social and political dimension. For him, the exploitation and oppression of the minjung by those who are wealthy and powerful is sin both against God and against humans. There are, of course, other types of sin defined as a violation of the law. However, Ahn argues that those kinds of sin are not determined by divine justice but defined according to the dominant value system established by the powers that be for the maintenance of the status quo.[25] Although he admits that the minjung are not without sin

21. Nam-dong Suh, "Confluence," 253.

22. Ahn, *Jesus of Galilee*, 188.

23. With respect to the political order, Ahn has a confidence in "the human self-governing possibilities of the minjung," and denies the unavoidability of a political order for human life. According to him, the political order is nothing but a disguise for the ruling class's will to domination, and, if there is no such oppressive order by the ruling power, "the autonomy of the minjung" is possible. Ahn, "Reply to the Theological Commission," 200–201.

24. Ahn, *Jesus of Galilee*, 188.

25. Ibid., 205.

in an ordinary moral sense, he nevertheless contends that they are not in need of forgiveness through any external agency.

Rejecting the efficacy of the vicarious atonement of Christ, Ahn calls such evangelical doctrine a paradox because, if we see it necessary for God to let Jesus be punished and die in place of humanity for their sins, then, according to Ahn, we cannot avoid regarding God himself as subject to the law of atonement itself.[26] According to him, the minjung can overcome moral failure through self-transcendence. By self-transcendence he means "the minjung's readiness to expend their efforts, their non-laziness, and their willingness for sacrifice."[27] In other words, they are considered to have the potential of self-transformation and self-liberation. Ahn, however, does not necessarily argue that the minjung can achieve their own liberation independently of God. For him, the self-transcendence of the minjung is worked out through the Holy Spirit, which he understands not as a person in the Trinity but as the divine power that can be found in every event of liberation. He thus maintains that God's work of salvation is not confined in Jesus but is freely extended beyond and outside of the Jesus event through the Holy Spirit.[28]

Denying the redemptive nature of the crucifixion of Jesus as divine atonement for humanity's sin, Ahn contends that in the crucifixion of Jesus "no deity was intervening."[29] For him, Jesus suffered and died not in a unique way as the Son of God, but in a way that epitomizes the suffering of the minjung. So Jesus is understood to have undergone "the same suffering" of the minjung "in the same condition" as the minjung suffer.[30] In the unjustly inflicted suffering and death of Jesus, according to Ahn, the minjung see their own suffering and their own death, and it is by this identification with Jesus that they come to realize that Jesus died "'for us,' 'for our sins,' and 'for our sake.'"[31] It is this realization of the minjung, Ahn argues, that makes Jesus the Messiah and establishes the essential tie between Jesus and the minjung.[32]

---

26. Ahn, *Discourse on Minjung Theology*, 91.
27. Ahn, "Reply to the Theological Commission," 205.
28. Ibid., 204; Ahn, *Discourse on Minjung Theology*, 220–21.
29. Ahn, *Jesus of Galilee*, 259.
30. Ibid.
31. Ibid., 258.
32. Ibid.

It was not so clear, however, to Jürgen Moltmann, a long-time supporter of minjung theology, in what way Ahn's identification of Jesus with the minjung was related to the actual deliverance of the minjung so the German theologian questions Ahn's Christology and asks who redeems the minjung if they are the Messiah.[33] Based on our discussion so far, Ahn's answer to this question may be simple: the minjung are not in need of a savior who is supposed to redeem them from their sin. For him, it is not the minjung who have the problem of sin that necessitates the saving work of the redeemer; it is the ruling class, who are guilty of injustice, which, according to him, can be redeemed by the suffering of the minjung. In this sense, Ahn interprets the suffering Servant of God in Isaiah 53 and the Lamb of God who takes away the sin of the world in John 1:29 to be the minjung.[34]

The fundamental problem of humanity, according to Ahn, is the social, political, and economic injustice caused by the sin of the ruling class only, and it has nothing to do with any sin in the religious dimension. For him, there is no religious sin in fact that taints human souls except for the ritual sin that is enacted by the ruling power as a way to manipulate the minjung. The minjung are considered to have no such sin in the traditional sense that separates them from God and, as a result, Ahn identifies the minjung with the people of God simply on the basis of their struggle for justice, regardless of receiving baptism or confessing faith in Christ.[35] From our observation so far it is clear that Ahn's theology operates on the *either/or* way of thinking with regard to the problem of sin. For him, the problem of sin is rooted only in exploitive human interrelationship caused by social and economic injustice, and not in human relation to God.[36]

The Scope of Sin

In their discussion of minjung theology, Byung-mu Ahn and Nam-dong Suh agree with each other that the injustice that the minjung have to suffer by the oppression of the ruling power constitutes the fundamental problem

---

33. Moltmann, *Experiences in Theology*, 259, 295–97.

34. Ahn, *Discourse on Minjung Theology*, 32–33. For the conversation between Ahn and Moltmann on this issue, see Moltmann, *Experiences in Theology*, 258–60.

35. Ahn, "Reply to the Theological Commission," 206–7.

36. Ahn talks about the sin of the ruling class against God, but it is always contingent on their sin against the minjung.

of humanity. They also concur in their emphasis on the social dimension of sin; for them, sin as the root of the human problem is social injustice. Suh differs from Ahn, however, with respect to the scope of sin. Both of them criticize the traditional concept of sin, which, according to them, is biased in such a way that it obscures sin as social injustice by overly focusing on sin as personal and religious transgression. Ahn replaces the traditional concept of sin with an exclusively political concept. Sin in a purely religious or personal ethical sense has no room in his thinking. In contrast, Suh by no means abandons the traditional notion of sin but wants to remedy it by putting a weightier emphasis on the long-neglected aspect of sin. He distinguishes between God's redemptive work in Christ and God's direct intervention in history through the Holy Spirit and contends that, though both aspects of the divine activity should be recognized, his minjung theology is a witness to the latter. Thus, he writes, "[I]n minjung theology we must give greater emphasis to the work of the Holy Spirit."[37] This view of Suh corresponds with Moltmann's criticism against Ahn.

In response to Ahn's rejection of the vicarious atonement of Christ, Moltmann concludes that Ahn's christology is unwarrantedly one-sided. In answering the question of the meaning of Jesus' death on Golgotha, he suggests two interpretations: The cross shows us God "*beside us* in our suffering" and God "*for us* in our guilt."[38] According to Moltmann, the former interpretation means "God's *solidarity* with us" in Christ as our brother, and thus is called "the inclusive solidarity christology"; the latter interpretation means "God's *atoning intervention* for us" in Christ as the redeemer, and so it is called "the exclusive representative Christology" or "the atonement Christology."[39] For Moltmann, the two Christologies are not necessarily opposing each other, nor should one be taken as an alternative to the other. Rather, one is inconceivable without presupposing the other.[40] According to Moltmann, however, Ahn maintains his minjung messianism as an inclusive solidarity Christology only in an exclusive way that denies the atonement Christology in which Christ is the personal redeemer.[41] In con-

37. Nam-dong Suh, "Historical References," 177.
38. Moltmann, *Jesus Christ*, 38.
39. Ibid., 38–42; Moltmann, *Experiences in Theology*, 256.
40. Moltmann, *Experiences in Theology*, 256. The New Testament, according to Moltmann's interpretation, supports both solidarity Christology and atonement Christology. Moltmann, *Jesus Christ*, 41.
41. Moltmann, *Experiences in Theology*, 256–59.

trast to Ahn, Suh does not reject the tradition christological interpretation that affirms Christ as the redeemer. He maintains his minjung theological interpretation of Christ in conjunction with the traditional atonement Christology and argues that the "two viewpoints are not antagonistic but supplementary."[42]

Suh, like Moltmann, considers the Messiah to be the one who not only identifies himself with the oppressed but also atones for the sins of the world. This shows that what he conceives of the human problem is not only the unjust suffering of the minjung from the oppressive and exploitive power relationships, but also universal human wrongdoing in its broad sense, including the sins that are considered purely religious and personal. To summarize, in developing his minjung theology, Suh gives a significant emphasis on the social and political dimension of human depravity as a fundamental aspect of the human problem, yet he still recognizes sin as wrongdoing in a religious or personal moral sense. With this conclusion, we now turn to Richard Mouw's understanding of what constitutes the fundamental human problem.

Richard Mouw's Understanding of the Human Problem

Politics and the Neo-Calvinist Worldview

This section discusses Richard Mouw's political theology in terms of how he conceives the fundamental human problem. In his book *Politics and the Biblical Drama*, Mouw offers a cogent discussion of his political theology from the neo-Calvinist worldview. Following the contemporary tendency of taking the meaning of the term *politics* in a broad sense, his political theology deals with "patterns of authority and access to decision-making power" in human interactions.[43] His theological reflection on political matters is informed essentially by the biblical message.[44] He emphasizes the neo-Calvinist worldview as being effectively and fundamentally grounded

42. Nam-dong Suh, "Historical References," 177.

43. Mouw, *Politics and the Biblical Drama*, 17.

44. There is a difference between Nam-dong Suh and Mouw with regard to the place of the Scriptures in their theologies. While Suh does not put an absolute normative priority on the Scriptures in his theological inquiry, Mouw does. So he contends, "If Christian theology is to be faithful to God's revelation of his will for his creation, it must center on the study of Holy Scripture." Ibid., 13.

in the biblical narrative.⁴⁵ For Mouw, Scripture cannot be considered a systematic discourse on any subject of human affairs, including political matters, but it does provide fundamental guidelines and criterion for every aspect of human living. So he observes:

> The Bible is the locus and record of God's address to human beings in their 'wholeness,' including the entire network of relationships, institutions, and projects in which they participate. The biblical message, then, addresses our political lives.⁴⁶

From Genesis to Revelation, according to him, the biblical narrative is in fact full of political concerns and the following are key examples: the Abrahamic covenant in the first book of Scripture, which includes promises of political well-being; the Exodus story of the liberation of the Hebrews from political oppression of Egypt; the psalmists' political prayers crying for justice; the prophets' political messages condemning social and political exploitation and injustice by the powerful; the temptation of political power Jesus faced; adn the apocalyptic vision infused with political themes in the last book of Scripture.⁴⁷ Considering the political concerns in the biblical narrative, politics cannot be simply regarded as a secular affair or a necessary evil, nor is it value neutral. Mouw sees the political structure of life from the neo-Calvinist worldview, which is shaped by the biblical metanarrative of *creation–fall–redemption–consummation*, and therefore considers it part of God's originally good creation, which, however, has been distorted by the perverting effect of the fall and is subject to redemption in Christ.

According to this approach, any consideration of human sin will be incomplete if it fails to take into account perversions in the political dimension of life; any understanding of God will also be inadequate if it precludes human political relationships from God's redemptive activity.⁴⁸ The all-encompassing nature of creation, fall, and redemption in the neo-

---

45. Calling attention to the tendency of the neo-Calvinist discussion of cultural transformation in a heavily philosophical and systematic-theological manner, Mouw presents his study on Isa 60 and contends that it is designed to "remedy this defect" by examining the *Christ and Culture* discussion from "the actual pages of the Bible." Mouw, *When Kings Come*, x.

46. Mouw, *Politics and the Biblical Drama*, 11.

47. Ibid., 10.

48. Ibid., 11. In this regard, Mouw argues that Christian witness should be directed toward a person in all of its relationships including political ones. See Mouw, *Political Evangelism*, 75–77.

Calvinist worldview is manifest in Mouw's view of how to consider and engage in political matters. This biblically informed worldview, however, inspires political thinking and involvement by providing principles rather than direct instructions. According to Mouw, scriptural guidance on political matters does not mean that one can expect to derive answers to specific political questions by simple deduction or inference from Scripture, but it means that one "must attempt to speak about political matters out of minds and hearts disciplined by the word from God."[49] As stated above, his discussion of human political interactions is based on the neo-Calvinist worldview and hence begins with the discussion of God's good creation.

Creation and Politics

Considering from the neo-Calvinist worldview, Thomas Hobbes's well-known account of the pure state of nature appears to begin only with the fall. He conceives of the natural condition of humankind as a state of *bellum omnium contra omnes* ("a war of all against all"), in which independent human beings fight against each other in their pursuit of power as there is no established political order.[50] Contrary to the Hobbesian proposal of the original state of nature, Mouw contends that "the 'original' condition is one of peace and harmony."[51] Hobbes's portrayal of human disposition as being selfish and power-driven is hardly disputable, and his view of the pure state of nature is still relevant with respect to international relationships among independent nations. The difference between the Hobbesian state of nature and Mouw's view is that Hobbes begins with the state of nature after the fall without due consideration of the pre-fallen state while Mouw begins with the original state of creation.

The natural condition of creation, according to Mouw, is that of *shalom* in every aspect of created reality. Human interrelationship, especially, was not in a state of *bellum omnium contra omnes* but was characterized by loving and orderly communion as the Creator intended it to be. After a short discussion on the "image of God" debates, Mouw concludes that, whether or not the image of God in the human person refers to sociality created into human nature in the likeness of God in Trinity, it is reasonable to think that social relationships are "a central dimension of human nature"

49. Ibid., 12.
50. Schmitt, *Leviathan*, 31, 92.
51. Mouw, *Politics and the Biblical Drama*, 30.

according to the biblical account of the creative will of God.[52] He contends that, along with this created sociality embedded in human nature, the political dimension in human social relationships is built into the creational order. In contrast to those who contend that political order is only a remedy for sinful disorders of human life after the fall, Mouw argues that politics should not be understood as "merely a post-fall phenomenon" but as "being rooted in the order of creation."[53]

Gordon Clark supports the idea that government and political order were alien to the original state of creation since they were later introduced to human life as a coercive order to regulate "a large number of evil people working at cross purposes."[54] John Howard Yoder also takes this line of view. Admitting that political order has been inevitable in human life since creation, Yoder, however, claims that it is essentially coercive and has "involved domination, disrespect for human dignity, and real or potential violence."[55] This is why he objects to Christian engagement in political activities.

According to Mouw, however, Yoder's view does not make a proper distinction between politics in the creational order and politics in the fallen order.[56] In opposition to Clark and Yoder, Mouw maintains that political order is part of good creation. For him, it is woven into the fabric of human life in accordance with the created human social nature. Following Kuyper, he argues that it is not the fall but creation from which political structures of human life originated. Without the fall, he asserts, human society would still have needed a political order, not as a safeguard against human perversity but as a "natural provision for regulating—'ordering'—the complexity of created cultural life."[57] Even without the occurrence of the fall, according to him, "some kind of hierarchy might have evolved."[58] By the term *hierarchy* he means authority structures that are necessary in human organizational relationships and he never means any hierarchy among humans that

---

52. Ibid., 28.

53. Ibid., 36.

54. Clark, *Christian View*, 138; quoted in Mouw, *Politics and the Biblical Drama*, 32 n. 14.

55. Yoder, *Politics of Jesus*, 203; quoted in Mouw, *Politics and the Biblical Drama*, 36 n. 19.

56. Mouw, *Politics and the Biblical Drama*, 35–36.

57. Mouw, *Abraham Kuyper*, 51.

58. Mouw, *Politics and the Biblical Drama*, 32.

is alleged to be natural. While agreeing with Kuyper in taking the political order as creational, Mouw, however, rejects Kuyper's suggestion that a hierarchical order is to be patterned by patriarchy.[59] For him, any kind of subordination, domination, or manipulation in human relationships is a perversion of the original order of creation.

In summary, Mouw sees political order as a natural development from the created human sociality that entails distribution of power and authority, decision-making, and accountability when a group of people interacts for a certain purpose. As grounded in the neo-Calvinist worldview, Mouw's political idealism from the perspective of creation is balanced with his political realism from the perspective of the fall.

Fall and Politics

Mouw sees sin as an ethical rebellion against God's will both in the human relationship with God and in their interpersonal relationships. In relation to his discussion of political theology from the neo-Calvinist worldview, Mouw emphasizes the radical and cosmic scope of the impact of the fall. Although the first sin was conceived in the human heart, its consequence is such that the entire order of creation and the whole person in all of its relationships have succumbed to the pervasive power of sin. With respect to the impact of sin on the wholeness of a human person, Mouw observes distortions in the three aspects of human consciousness identified by developmental psychologists: affection, volition, and cognition. According to him, sin distorts the ways one feels, wills, and thinks as the process of the fall in the Genesis account demonstrates.[60]

Along with the perversions that can be seen in all human faculties, the fall manifests its effects on human life in "all idolatrous and prideful attachments to military, technological, commercial, and cultural might," and "all of those rebellious projects which glorify oppression, exploitation, and the accumulation of possessions."[61] According to Mouw, the fall has impacted not just the human soul but also social structures and processes in such a way that simple renewal of personal lives will not automatically result in social and political reforms.[62] Against the conservative Christian belief

59. Ibid., 34–35.
60. Mouw, *Distorted Truth*, 33.
61. Mouw, *When the Kings Come*, 18–19.
62. Mouw, *Political Evangelism*, 15–16.

that "changed hearts will change society," he argues that without changing "the manipulative patterns which are built into the very structures of social relationships" genuine change will not be possible.[63]

Mouw draws attention to how personal and social ethics are related to each other. Rebellion against the Creator at a personal level, according to him, is the root of all kinds of injustice and oppression in human social relationships, and an unjust and oppressive social order is how personal rebellion is institutionalized.[64] Without understanding the personal dimension of human rebellion in attempting to be like God, one cannot properly understand human desire to manipulate others for selfish gain and the distorted social relationships as its inevitable result. At the same time, without recognizing the perverting power of sin embedded in social relationships, one cannot fully understand the far-reaching impacts of personal rebellion against God's will. In this sense, Mouw contends that when personal rebellion is institutionalized it is no longer a matter of personal choice but can go beyond an individual's control. This is why the good will of individual persons cannot remove systemic injustice and oppression without changing the social order into which these evils are built.

Although Mouw here does not refer to Reinhold Niebuhr, he clearly resonates with Niebuhr's view of institutionalized evil in human collective life, which he deals with in his book *Moral Man and Immoral Society*. Individual persons, according to Niebuhr, can engage in self-criticism and have a moral capacity to go beyond their self-interest in making moral choices, but nations and social classes operate differently: they can hardly transcend their collective egoism.[65] The dominant classes always pursue their own interest and rarely yield their privileges for common good unless they are checked by countervailing social power. For this reason, Niebuhr claims that coercive measures by political power are necessary to achieve social justice. Niebuhr's realist approach is different from Mouw's transformationalist approach, but the two thinkers show a common observation that injustice and oppression are not something that are occasionally perpetrated by some wicked people, but are something structurally incorporated into the social fabric. Mouw, in this sense, argues that institutionalized injustice and oppression in human collective

---

63. Mouw, *Politics and the Biblical Drama*, 49–50. See also Mouw, *When the Kings Come*, 64.

64. Ibid., 49.

65. Reinhold Niebuhr, *Moral Man*, 25, 88.

life "can come to have a life of their own."[66] For him, therefore, simple acts of charity are not enough to solve social problems, but structural approaches and collective actions are required.

The Two Kingdom Approach

According to Mouw, human sin as a rebellion against the Creator is manifested in both human personal and social life, and in both the spiritual and the political realms of life. This holistic approach to the fundamental human problem is contrasted by VanDrunen's dualist approach. As we discussed earlier, VanDrunen maintains that the current order of things is divided into the temporal civil kingdom and the spiritual kingdom of Christ, with the former excluded from the redemptive work of Christ. Interpreting Christ's redemption as affecting only the spiritual kingdom, VanDrunen holds that renewal of the civil kingdom is not a goal of the redemption Christ inaugurated in his death and resurrection.[67] It is not that he has no appreciation of anything that belongs to the civil kingdom or does not take evil in the society seriously. In fact, he promotes Christian social engagement and considers it a Christian moral responsibility ordained by God. What distinguishes him from the neo-Calvinist approach is that he denies the redemptive nature of Christian social engagement. For him, seeking justice through political activities is a matter of the civil kingdom, not of Christ's redemptive kingdom.[68] He argues that Christian activities for social justice and peace should not be understood or pursued as a distinctively Christian task but as a general moral task for all people to advance common good of the society according to common moral standards.[69] For him, the common good of society or social justice, no matter how necessary it may be for the common life on earth, relates to the temporal order and is separated from God's redemptive providence. The order of the civil kingdom is still a good order ordained by God, according to VanDrunen, but

---

66. Mouw, *Politics and the Biblical Drama*, 49.

67. According to the two kingdoms doctrine that VanDrunen proposes, "God is *not redeeming* the cultural activities and institutions of this world, but is *preserving* them through the covenant he made with all living creatures through Noah in Gen 8:20—9:17." With regard to the redemption in Christ, VanDrunen contends that "God is *redeeming* a people for himself by virtue of the covenant made with Abraham . . ." VanDrunen, *Living in God's Two Kingdoms*, 15 (italics original).

68. Ibid,, 194–95.

69. Ibid., 204.

ANTHROPOLOGICAL COMPARISON: WHAT IS THE HUMAN PROBLEM?

does not require any uniquely Christian dealing with it except when a clear command of God given in the Scriptures is obviously violated by the civil kingdom.[70] For him, Christ's kingdom goes in parallel with the civil kingdom and keeps distance from it. While the two kingdoms are both good orders governed by God, he understands them as mutually exclusive; the civil kingdom and the kingdom of God do not in principle allow any interaction between them that is intended to effect change in the other.

When he contends that Christ's redemption has nothing to do with the civil kingdom, VanDrunen shows that he has a dualistic understanding of the fundamental human problem. According to him, Christ in his redemption has initiated his kingdom here and now by renewing the human heart and restoring their relationship with God. Restoration of the human social and political life by eliminating oppression and injustice, in contrast, has to wait until the eschatological kingdom drastically replaces the current civil kingdom because, for him, the redemptive work of Christ is not supposed to change anything in society.[71] In this way of thinking, the human problem is separable into spiritual and social predicaments, and the latter is always considered of secondary importance; sin as spiritual alienation from God is regarded as something that needs urgent care, but sin as social alienation and injustice is treated as something that has to be endured in this life of spiritual pilgrimage. In contrast to this approach, Mouw shows an integrated and holistic approach to the human problem. For him, the spiritual and the social problems are so inseparably intertwined that a genuine remedy for them must deal with both of them simultaneously.[72] Though he takes both spiritual alienation from God and social injustice as constituting the essential human problem, he does not propose that a complete social renewal is possible in this world. Yet, to say that the present social order will

---

70. Ibid., 199–203. He takes problems of abortion, marriage, and war as examples of the political issues about which the Scriptures provide many relevant teachings. With respect to supporting or objecting concrete political and public policies regarding the issues, he contends that individual Christians should be allowed to use their own discretion and conscience. When the issue involves clear violation of a scriptural command and its required resolution is so obvious, then, according to him, the church may have to speak in a specifically Christian voice. It is interesting, however, that he does not give any attention to the issue of poverty and social injustice, about which the Scriptures give far more relevant teachings and commands.

71. For VanDrunen, improvement of social and political conditions belongs to the civil kingdom, which is the realm of natural law and has no bearing in redemption in Christ. See Ibid., 15, 56–62; VanDrunen, *Natural Law*, 113.

72. Mouw, *Political Evangelism*, 16–17.

not be fundamentally transformed before the eschatological consummation is one thing; and to say that it is in need of redemptive transformation is another. Mouw maintains that both spiritual and social disorders are the root of the fundamental human problem, and that both of them must be subject to the redemptive restoration in Christ.

To summarize, Mouw sees political order as originating from the creational order and authorities in political relationships as essential for that order. The perverting impact of the fall in all dimensions of human life, however, causes distortions in power and authority relationships too. Not only the human soul but also all human relationships including political relationships are under the influence of sinful distortion. Further, perversions in the political order appears as injustice and oppression toward the powerless, which is systemically built into institutional relationships and societal structures. For Mouw, social injustice and oppression permeate so deeply and so subtly into the structural dimension of human existence that any effort to eliminate them must involve changing not just individual hearts but the social order itself. Equipped with this understanding, we now turn to the comparison of Mouw and Suh in their understanding of the fundamental human problem.

Similarities and Differences

Nam-dong Suh's minjung theology and Richard Mouw's neo-Calvinist political theology have a shared diagnosis of the human problem. For both theologians, human beings are dehumanized and their social life falls short of God's creative purpose due to the injustice and oppression that are deep-seated in human collective relationships.[73] They take social injustice seriously and consider it a fundamental problem that the Christian message must address. For Suh, oppression toward the minjung is such an essential issue in theology that without due consideration of the minjung's suffering one cannot have true knowledge of Jesus.[74] Mouw also contends that the advent of Jesus was "a threat to the political status quo" and that the new life Jesus brings is "a new *political* life."[75] Concerning the moral status of the

---

73. Like Mouw, Suh also recognizes that the structural themes of the biblical narrative are creation, fall, and redemption. Nam-dong Suh, *Theology at a Turning Point*, 104.

74. Nam-dong Suh, *Study in Minjung Theology*, 211.

75. Mouw, *Political Evangelism*, 24–25 (italics original).

ANTHROPOLOGICAL COMPARISON: WHAT IS THE HUMAN PROBLEM?

minjung or the oppressed, however, they show a difference between each other that demands our attention.

Moral Status of the Oppressed

Suh underscores the injustice of the ruling power in manipulating and victimizing the minjung. He gives more emphasis on social immorality than the personal violations of moral laws and thus argues that the minjung are not sinners in the traditional moral sense but victims who are sinned against by the ruling classes. This view is not alien to neo-Calvinist thinking. Wolterstorff makes a similar note in his Kuyper Lecture. Citing two Old Testament passages, he argues that in a society where there is a division between the poor and the rich God is "on the side of the poor, for it is they, [God] says, who are being wronged."[76] He continues, "To be impoverished is to fall short of shalom. *That* is what is wrong with poverty."[77] If sin is defined as falling short of God's will for his creation, which is shalom, then the problem of poverty is not merely an economic problem but a problem of sin. In this line of thinking, any individual or social system that causes and perpetuates poverty can be held sinful. "The wickedness of the rich and the powerful," Mouw observes, "regularly manifests itself in the form of sins against the poor and oppressed."[78] Therefore, according to him, Christians are called to confront oppressions and to identify themselves with the poor and oppressed.[79]

Mouw, however, does not simply regard the poor and oppressed as innocent victims. While the sinful distortion of human relationships is evident in the manipulation of the powerless by the powerful, he also holds that it can also be manifest in the condition of the powerless who are being manipulated. For him, not only the desire to become a coercive "lord" over others but also voluntarily allowing others to assume the role of manipulative "lords" over themselves show the dehumanizing effects of sin.[80] Mouw's point here may be best understood by an example of people who live under tyranny and willingly submit to coercive rule. Considering the suggestion of Jean-Paul Sartre and others that both masochism and

---

76. Wolterstorff, *Until Justice and Peace*, 76.
77. Ibid., 77 (italics original).
78. Mouw, *Politics and the Biblical Drama*, 80.
79. Ibid., 70–72.
80. Ibid., 48–49.

sadism can be forms of "bad faith," Mouw contends that both desiring to be a manipulator and allowing oneself to be manipulated constitute falling short of the Creator's intention for humanness.[81]

He never implies, however, that being manipulated is always accompanied by a voluntary submission to coercive power. On the contrary, he recognizes that it is the wickedness of the rich and powerful that violates the rights of the powerless in oppressive and manipulative ways. Yet, his emphasis is on the fact that the distortive power of sin can be found in all human beings regardless of their social and political status in such a way that even the oppressed cannot claim to be free from the pervasive influence of sin. In this respect, he observes, "Indeed, it is unlikely that there have been many human beings who have simply been oppressed without also engaging in oppression of their own."[82] For Mouw, it is possible that there is a minjung who is oppressive to other minjung. If the tax collectors in the Gospel accounts are to be considered minjung in any sense, for example, from the viewpoint of the Roman rulers and the Jewish religious power, then they can be an example of minjung who oppress and exploit other minjung.[83] This difference between Suh and Mouw regarding the moral vulnerability of the minjung is closely related to another difference between them regarding the cause of injustice and oppression.

The Origin of Injustice

For Suh, it is from the institutionalization and concentration of power that social injustice and oppression toward the powerless originated. Mouw, in contrast, traces the human problem back to the personal rebellion against the Creator in the fall. It is from perversion in the personal heart, according to him, that all kinds of distortion in human relationships stem. Their difference with regard to the origin of injustice then leads to their different views on the moral status of the oppressed. For Suh, it is the monopolization of power that has produced injustice against the powerless, and therefore it is not the powerless but the powerful that are responsible

---

81. Ibid.

82. Ibid., 49. One can be an oppressed victim in one relationship with others while being an oppressor in another relationship. For Mouw, therefore, a simple dichotomy of the oppressors and the oppressed cannot be an adequate analysis for human relationships under the sinful distortion.

83. See Seyoon Kim, "Is 'Minjung Theology,'" 264.

for the social evil as the fundamental human problem. Mouw, in contrast, pays more serious attention to the perversion of the human heart as the root cause of distorted human relationships and thus points out that one can be both a perpetrator and a victim of injustice at the same time depending on one's relationship with others. However, their difference is not such that Suh finds the cause of the human problem only in the structural and Mouw only in the personal.

Mouw maintains that the problem of social injustice cannot be reduced to the wickedness of some individual persons. For him, the personal and spiritual rebellion against God's creative purpose for human beings cannot be effectively separated from systemic injustice in human collective life. For this reason, he contends that Christian witness must address not only the spiritual needs of individual persons but also social and political injustice. "The anger and frustration of the victim of racial prejudice or political oppression," he observes, "can often make it practically impossible for [the victim] to listen to the Christian message."[84]

With regard to Suh, he focuses almost exclusively on structural injustice and the *Han* of the minjung as the fundamental human problem. Nevertheless, he still recognizes the problem of sin as an essential human problem. It is an illusion, he argues, to suppose that one can save oneself. Self-salvation is impossible, according to him, because human beings are under the bondage of sin, and thus have lost self-determination. For him, it is not what existentialists call self-determination but a divine intervention that makes human self-transcendence possible.[85]

In summary, Suh gives considerable emphasis to injustice and oppression in human institutional relationships as the fundamental human problem, yet he does not ignore the religious dimension of the human problem. Mouw takes the fall as the root of the human problem, and yet he understands human rebellion in the fall as inevitably perverting human social existence. Their difference, then, can be understood as a methodological one. in his formulation of minjung theology, Suh is concerned primarily with identifying the meaning of the minjung's suffering, and thus his approach is social and historical as well as theological. This is evident from the fact that he uses Scripture and the Korean minjung tradition as equally important sources for his theology.[86] Suh pays greater attention to the analysis of the

---

84. Mouw, *Political Evangelism*, 17.

85. Nam-dong Suh, *Study in Minjung Theology*, 418.

86. Nam-dong Suh, "Historical References," 177; idem, *Study in Minjung Theology*, 184.

life of the minjung and their theological significance than to the theological understanding of injustice and its origin.

In contrast, Mouw considers politics from the perspective of *creation–fall–redemption–consummation* in the neo-Calvinist worldview. His discussion of the problem of injustice, therefore, traces back to the political order in creation and its perversion in the fall. For this reason, while Suh focuses on the minjung's experience of injustice and oppression as the ultimate human problem, Mouw goes further to their religious root in the fall. This theoretical approach of Mouw could prevent him from taking the real human situation seriously enough because it can be perceived only from experience. However, as the following chapters show, Mouw consistently pays serious attention to social and political injustice and redemptive involvement to remove it. In fact, his conceptual approach need not to oppose Suh's approach but can be complemented by Suh's experience-based and practice-oriented approach as this study suggests.

The Both/And Approach

Suh and Mouw seem to show a difference with regard to what constitutes the fundamental human problem, but it is basically a matter of emphasis and, for the most part, derives from their difference in theological method. In reality, as the above discussion already implied, Suh is closer to Mouw than to his fellow minjung theologian Byung-mu Ahn in his understanding of the essential human problem. Mouw, too, is closer to Suh than to such Reformed theologians as VanDrunen in his affirmation that structural injustice and oppression toward the powerless are essential problems that the Christian message should address in relation to the redemption in Christ.

What makes Suh's and Mouw's theologies close to each other and mutually acceptable in their understanding of the essential human problem is based on the inclusive *both/and* way of thinking they share. In contrast to Ahn, who gives his exclusive attention to social injustice as the single source of the human problem, and VanDrunen, who excludes the social life from the life-changing redemptive activity of Christ, Suh and Mouw take both spiritual disorder and social injustice as the fundamental human problem. They do not choose one over against the other but take both aspects of the human problem seriously. This makes their theological reflections in this matter compatible with each other and mutually acceptable.

ANTHROPOLOGICAL COMPARISON: WHAT IS THE HUMAN PROBLEM?

In this way of thinking, even though they have different focuses and different emphases, their theologies can complement, instead of reject, each other. As already pointed out, Suh's radical focus on social injustice and Mouw's comprehensive understanding of human fallenness are not only reconcilable with each other but they can balance and reinforce each other's perspective. Without dealing with specific social injustice and oppression in real life, a comprehensive explanation of reality, no matter how intelligible it may be, cannot practically bring about transformation. In the same way, a radical concern for social justice cannot effect fundamental transformation without serious theological consideration of the root of human fallenness. Consequently, we can consider the different focuses of Suh and Mouw in respect of their *both/and* way of thinking. Their different focuses need not be contradictory or alternative to each other but can be complementary. Suh's focus on liberation from injustice and Mouw's holistic approach to human fallenness can complement each other as different but equally important emphases in understanding the fundamental human problem.

In conclusion, despite their methodological difference, Suh and Mouw show significant agreement with each other in their understanding of the fundamental human problem. As a result, Suh's minjung theology and Mouw's neo-Calvinist political theology can be considered compatible with each other in this respect. While they are in line with each other in their assessment of the human problem, a more critical test for their theological compatibility will be the one regarding their proposed answers to the problem. Hence, we now turn to the comparison of their christological understandings with respect to their transformational visions.

6

Christological Comparison: Who Is Jesus?

Jesus went on with his disciples to the villages of Caesarea Philippi; and on the way he asked his disciples, "Who do people say that I am?" And they answered him, "John the Baptist; and others, Elijah; and still others, one of the prophets." He asked them, "But who do you say that I am?" Peter answered him, "You are the Messiah."
(Mark 8:27–29)

AN ANSWER TO THE question of who Jesus is characterizes one's theology definitively. A christological consideration, therefore, is crucial in comparing two theological thoughts. This chapter compares Nam-dong Suh and Richard Mouw in terms of how they conceive of Jesus in their theological visions of social transformation. Two questions are crucial: what kind of Messiah is Jesus, and how does he bring about transformation? The first question is inevitably linked with a question of what kind of transformation Christ is up to and thus deals with the nature and scope of transformation Christ brings. The second question concerns the agent of transformation and thus deals with the relation of Christ's initiative and human responsibility in transformation. It is a general assumption among Korean theologians that the christological understanding of minjung theology and Reformed theology is so different from each other that they share almost no agreement on their view of the person and work of Christ. The two theological camps criticize each other as portraying Christ as an occult savior or a political revolutionary.

This chapter shows that Suh's rendition of minjung theology and Mouw's Reformed political theology share significant agreement on the aforementioned christological questions. For both of them, Christ is not a political liberator who has no concern for spiritual dimension of salvation or a savior of the soul who has no vision for social transformation. Rather, they employ the *both/and* way of thinking and maintain that the work of Christ brings transformation in both spiritual and political dimensions of life. With regard to the question of how transformation is worked out, they also show an agreement in rejecting both a human-endeavor-alone approach and a socially irresponsible pietistic approach. Instead, they argue that divine activity works along with human cooperation for the holistic transformation, which inaugurated in the death and resurrection of Christ. Based on this observation, it is clear that Suh and Mouw engage in their theological reflections of the person and work of Christ in a *both/and* way of thinking. For them, the fundamental change that Christ brings affects both personal and social life and both the human relationships with God and with fellow humans. They also agree that both divine agency and human agency are actively involved in cooperation for the messianic transformation of society. This inclusive *both/and* approach of the two theologians allows their understandings of the radical transformation in Christ to be comparable with each other and mutually acceptable.

For a detailed discussion of Suh's answer to the two christological questions, we will look at his minjung messianism in contrast to Ahn's minjung messianism. For Mouw's answer, we will examine his understanding of the nature and scope of redemption in Christ from the perspective of the neo-Calvinist worldview, and his view of the Christian community in relation to Christ's redemptive activity in the world. Mouw's view will be discussed in contrast to VanDrunen's two kingdoms perspective. When contrasted to the *either/or* approach of Ahn and VanDrunen, the inclusive *both/and* approach of Suh and Mouw and their theological affinity based on that will become more evident.

Nam-dong Suh's Minjung Messianism

Suh argues that Jesus is "the personification of the minjung and their symbol"[1] and that "the subject matter of minjung theology is not Jesus but the minjung."[2] This makes Moltmann suspicious of Suh's Christology as infelicitously reductionistic if it takes the significance of Jesus only as a collective symbol for the minjung.[3] Seyoon Kim also criticizes Suh for denying the salvific work of Jesus for the minjung and for advocating instead

1. Nam-dong Suh, "Historical References," 159.
2. Ibid., 160.
3. Moltmann, *Experiences in Theology*, 259.

a doctrine of self-salvation, which, according to him, is merely a sociopolitical liberation.[4] In contrast, Tae-soo Yim contends that Suh regards Jesus as the Lord of redemption and an object of faith.[5] According to Yim, Suh shows significant differences from Ahn in his christological understanding. In fact, Suh affirms the traditional christological statement that Jesus of Nazareth atoned for the sins of humanity by becoming their substitute in his death.[6]

There is thus ambiguity in Suh's christological discussion that causes different and sometimes even opposing interpretations of his theology. In order to get a clearer picture of his christological understanding, we must distinguish his minjung messianism from that of Byung-mu Ahn. The confusion and misunderstanding in discussions about Suh's Christology are due largely to the failure in recognizing the difference between Suh's and Ahn's Christology. Ahn and Suh maintain different christological understandings from each other even when they use the same language. When they say, "The minjung are the Messiah," Ahn and Suh do not agree about the same thing. Some critics, however, convey undiscriminating criticism to Suh without paying adequate attention to the difference between Suh and Ahn in their minjung messianism. For example, Young-han Kim argues that both Suh and Ahn identify the minjung with Jesus and view the crucifixion of Jesus only as a political event.[7] When criticizing Suh's Christology, they assume his view as the same as Ahn's and thus commit the straw man fallacy in their argument. Those interpretations of Suh do not do justice to his Christology. In order to get a fair view of Suh's christological understanding in distinction from Ahn's, we will first look at Ahn's minjung messianism, which most critics of minjung theology assume as the general Christology of minjung theology. Against the backdrop of Ahn's Christology, we will then discuss Suh's minjung messianism to see how distinctive his Christology is from Ahn's.

---

4. Seyoon Kim, "Is 'Minjung Theology,'" 261, 272.

5. Yim, "Nam-dong Suh's Understanding," 121–22.

6. Nam-dong Suh, "Confluence," 272. He uses the words "for me" and "in my place" in describing the atoning death of Jesus. In another place, when he talks about the meaning of salvation, he clearly states, "Although we were sinners, God justified us in Christ and reconciled us with himself. Through the death of Christ God granted us the state of being reconciled, which is salvation." Nam-dong Suh, *Theology at a Turning Point*, 103.

7. Young-han Kim, "Problems with Minjung Theology," paras. 14–16. See also Young-han Kim et al., "Forum."

Byung-mu Ahn's Minjung Messianism

Ahn's Christology is based on his understanding of the historical Jesus rather than on the *kerygma* of the New Testament. He distinguishes the *kerygma* in the New Testament from the account of what he calls the Jesus event in the Synoptic Gospels, arguing that the former is a subjective dogmatic principle abstracted by the leadership of the institutionalized church for an apologetic purpose, while the latter is an objective, historical account of what actually happened to the minjung.[8] According to him, the description of the death of Jesus in the *kerygma* as a vicarious sacrifice and a fulfillment of the Old Testament messianic prophesies is not founded on the historical truth of the Jesus event.[9] He argues that the *kerygma* is not just void of the true information about what really happened, but actually distorts the truth of the Jesus event by providing biased descriptions.[10] "[T]he historical event of Jesus was made abstract by being proclaimed kerygmatically," he insists, "connoting only its meaning instead of describing it as it happened."[11] One possible reason for this, according to him, is that the leadership of the early church "tried to avoid the minjung's armed resistance by sublimating the minjung's hostility into spirituality."[12]

The core of the Jesus event, according to Ahn, is the fact that Jesus was crucified as a political criminal against Rome in the midst of the political power game between the ruling authorities of Jerusalem and Rome.[13] The minjung of Galilee, then, found their own fate in Jesus, who suffered and was executed as a result of political persecution by the powers that be. Reflecting their own suffering and hope in what they witnessed in the Jesus event, a certain group of the minjung transmitted the oral tradition of the Jesus event based on concrete historical experiences. The apostolic church leadership, on the contrary, formulated the Christ *kerygma* by abstracting and dogmatizing the story of the passion and resurrection of Jesus to emphasize only the spiritual redemption and triumph at the expense of the political significance of the event. Thus, Ahn contends that the historical depiction of the Jesus event by the minjung was fundamentally different

---

8. Ahn, "Transmitters of the Jesus-Event," 29–30.
9. Ibid., 31.
10. Ibid., 35; idem, *Jesus of Galilee*, 224.
11. Ahn, "Transmitters of the Jesus-Event," 34.
12. Ibid.
13. Ibid., 37.

from the preaching of the *kerygma* that focused on the proclamation of Jesus as the Christ.[14]

Ahn blatantly rejects the *kerygma* of the New Testament as a biased source that is not adequate for understanding who Jesus really is. Instead, in pursuing the historical Jesus he insists that the true portrayal of the historical Jesus can be found in the Jesus event tradition transmitted by the minjung in the form of rumor and included mostly in Mark's Gospel and limitedly in Matthew and Luke.[15] According to this tradition, the story of Jesus, including the passion narrative, does not depict a heroic triumph of Jesus as the Christ, but rather the suffering, cry, and hope of the minjung.[16] What is distinctive in Ahn's Christology is that he finds the significance of Jesus in his sufferings as a collective symbol for the minjung rather than in what he did as an individual person. He interprets the life of Jesus as a "socio-biography" of the minjung and the passion narrative as a climax of the minjung's suffering.[17] Thus, concerning the passion narrative in Mark, he observes, "Drawing on the history of Jesus' passion, Mark is telling the suffering history of the minjung of his own time. And conversely, Jesus' suffering is 'actualized' in the fate of the minjung at the time when Mark was writing."[18] For Ahn, therefore, it was not Jesus of Nazareth but the minjung as a collective entity that was deserted, subjected to unjust trials, and persecuted to the point of death on the cross. If the minjung understood that Jesus died *for* them, it was in the sense that Jesus embodied their own death. In the same way, the resurrection of Jesus, according to Ahn, signifies the resurrection of the Galilean minjung, who were as good as dead with despair.[19] Ahn's focus on the minjung rather than the person Jesus is also obvious in his understanding of the healing stories in the Gospels.

14. Ibid., 38, 47.

15. Ibid., 35, 39, 47; idem, "Jesus and *Ochlos*," 89, 95. Ahn argues that Matthew and Luke distorted the original message in Mark about Jesus' attitude toward the minjung. In Mark, according to him, Jesus never rebukes the minjung nor does he demand repentance from them. Ahn's understanding of the Jesus-Event is grounded chiefly in his interpretation of Mark, and yet he contends that Mark is also compromised by the Christ *kerygma*. Seyoon Kim criticizes these arguments as exegetically inconsistent and arbitrarily romanticizing the minjung; Seyoon Kim, "Is 'Minjung Theology,'" 260-71.

16. Ahn, "Transmitters of the Jesus-Event," 39-44.

17. Ahn, "Subject of History," 183-84; Moltmann, *Experiences in Theology*, 259.

18. Ahn, in Moltmann ed., *Minjung Theologie des Volkes Gottes in Südkorea* (Neukirchen, 1984), 167; quoted in Moltmann, *Experiences in Theology*, 259.

19. Ahn, "Subject of History," 183-84.

CHRISTOLOGICAL COMPARISON: WHO IS JESUS?

The miracle stories in the Gospels, Ahn maintains, are not intended to reveal the identity of Jesus as having divine power and authority. They are rather intended to show the liberation experience of those who were physically ill, materially deprived, and politically persecuted (he suggests that the suffering from demon possession was caused by political oppression), and those who suffered from various social injustice due to their powerlessness. Reflected in the miracle stories, according to him, is "not only the [economic] motive of the poor and the social motive of the alienated, but also their political hope."[20] For him, one may miss the main purpose of the miracle stories if she seeks to find any eschatological, christological, or soteriological significance in them because essential to the stories are the suffering of the minjung and their liberation from it rather than the question of who Jesus is.[21]

Rejecting the *kerygma* of the New Testament and regarding Jesus as a collective symbol for the minjung, Ahn holds radically different understanding of Jesus from traditional Christology. He plainly denies the two natures of Christ as an espousal of a Greco-Roman idea that is no longer valid.[22] Criticizing the vicarious atonement of the traditional Christology, he argues that Jesus never claimed to die for the sake of sinners, nor did he understand his death as an atoning sacrifice.[23] In this regard, Ahn once suggested renaming Communion to "common meal" to remove the sacrificial and redemptive dimension from the sacrament.[24] For him, Jesus is not the redeemer or the Messiah in an exclusive way, and he never thought of himself as the Messiah. Instead, Ahn contends that the minjung are the Messiah who will save the world and bring in the ultimate kingdom of God. The way the minjung can save the world, according to him, is their endurance of the sufferings that are unjustly inflicted on them. They bear the sufferings even though they did nothing that deserved the sufferings. For Ahn, the sufferings are caused by the evil of the world that the minjung have nothing to do with, but the minjung are forced to bear the unmerited sufferings. In this regard, the suffering of the minjung, he argues, is *for* the world, and they are the Lamb of God who takes away the sins of the world.[25] According to him, the minjung do not resist or revenge those who

20. Ahn, "Transmitters of the Jesus-Event," 43.
21. Ibid., 44.
22. Ahn, *Discourse on Minjung Theology*, 87.
23. Ibid., 89.
24. Jin-Ho Kim, "Hermeneutics of Ahn," 17, n. 8.
25. Ahn, *Discourse on Minjung Theology*, 32–33.

oppress them and cause sufferings on them, but they just endure their sufferings. This is how they remove the sins of the world: refusing to revenge against evil and choosing instead to forgive the oppressors, they can break the vicious circle of vengeance and take the initiative to build up a new relationship of reconciliation.[26]

This perspective finds a parallel in Martin Luther King Jr. Recalling his encounter with King during the civil rights movement in the early 1960s, Syngman Rhee observes that King's activism was based on his conviction that "the key to the creation of a new history lies in the hands of the oppressed and suffering people."[27] As the oppressed choose to forgive the oppressors for a new reconciled relationship, the suffering of the oppressed is not just an evil to overcome but it also serves as a means to make the oppressors shamefully see their injustice. According to Rhee, King called this suffering of the oppressed "vicarious suffering" and, for this reason, he believed that the civil rights movement was intended to liberate both the black oppressed and the white oppressors.[28] This is analogical to how Ahn sees the suffering of the minjung.

Jesus, according to Ahn, did not resist the sword with the sword but swallowed up the sword of the oppressors in his death. Once he willingly suffered, submitting himself even to the point of death, those who inflicted the suffering with the sword and violence can no longer stand and their wickedness is disclosed.[29] For Ahn, however, the death of Jesus is not a death of an individual person but the death of the minjung, who were oppressed by the ruling power. The significance of Jesus, then, is in the fact that he embodied the suffering of the Galilean minjung in a climactic way and exposed the injustice of the ruling classes of his time vividly. Consequently, Ahn does not see the Jesus event as a unique, once-and-for-all event occurred in a particular time and place in the past. For him, it is the minjung movement for liberation that repeatedly takes place in different ways throughout history. In summary, Ahn rejects all religious implications in the suffering and death of Jesus and interprets the life of Jesus only as an embodiment of the suffering, despair, and hope of the minjung in overcoming their fate and finding themselves as an instrument for the salvation of the world.

26. Ibid., 96.
27. Rhee, "Reconciliation," 73.
28. Ibid., 73–74.
29. Ahn, "Subject of History," 184.

Nam-dong Suh's Minjung Messianism

Similar to Ahn, Nam-dong Suh also maintains that the minjung are the Messiah. However, his minjung messianism shows remarkable differences from Ahn's. The most notable difference is that, for Suh, the minjung play a messianic *role* in the salvation of the world while Ahn identifies the minjung with the Messiah. Suh takes up two parables of Jesus to argue how the minjung play a messianic role. In the parable of the Good Samaritan in Luke 10, the one who plays the messianic role, according to him, is not the Good Samaritan as in the traditional interpretation, but the person who is beaten, robbed, and left half-dead along the road.[30] The groan of the victim, Suh contends, is the call of the Messiah, and the response to the former is the response to the later.[31] The Samaritan, in that case, does not represent the Messiah who saves but rather those who are being saved by responding to the cry of the suffering, who are in fact playing the role of the Messiah. According to Suh, then, it is not the minjung themselves but the suffering they undergo that plays the messianic role; "By taking part in the suffering of the minjung," he says, "one becomes true human being and, in that way, she is saved."[32] In line of this interpretation, the priest and the Levite who just passed by on the other side in this parable indicate religious people without deeds. Thus, it is implied that religiously devoted people who ignore the suffering of the minjung are in reality rejecting the Messiah. Suh discusses another parable of Jesus to make his point clearer.

Suh takes the parable of the Sheep and the Goats in Matthew 25:31–46 as supporting his minjung messianism. In this parable Jesus identifies himself with those who are afflicted and disadvantageous, a kind of people usually identified as the minjung in minjung theology. Discussing the parable, Suh contends that the minjung are the Messiah in the sense that Jesus "the Messiah comes to us in the guise of the oppressed minjung."[33] Quoting the saying of Jesus in verse 40, which reads, "Truly I tell you, just as

---

30. Nam-dong Suh, *Study in Minjung Theology*, 180–82; idem, "Envisagement of Han," 344. When he mentions the traditional interpretation of the parable, Suh must be referring to the allegorical interpretation that was prevalent in the early Christianity. In such interpretation the Samaritan represents Jesus who saves the soul fallen into the hand of Satan. Suh, however, does not seem to consider the fact that such interpretation has been largely discredited as irrelevant to the original purpose and meaning of the parable.

31. Nam-dong Suh, "Envisagement of Han," 344.

32. Nam-dong Suh, *Study in Minjung Theology*, 181.

33. Ibid., 217.

you did it to one of the least of these who are members of my family, you did it to me," he argues that to serve the minjung is to serve Jesus. Further, though he does not explicitly quote Jesus' saying in verse 45, which reads, "Truly I tell you, just as you did not do it to one of the least of these, you did not do it to me," he must be reasoning on the basis of that verse when he argues that to refuse to identify with the suffering minjung is to repeat the failure of Judaism of rejecting Jesus as the Messiah due to its false expectation about the Promised One.[34]

Jesus is present, according to Suh, not only in the sacramental bread and cup but also in suffering neighbors. "While we are given the grace of the atonement of the Lord by partaking of the bread and wine in the Communion," he argues, "by standing in solidarity with our neighbors in their suffering and *han*, we are given the redemptive grace of receiving Christ who brings in the new age"; and he finds in this process "a messianic characteristic of the suffering minjung."[35] Unlike Ahn, who equates the minjung with the Messiah, Suh does not take the minjung to be the same as the Messiah. For him, Jesus the Messiah is unambiguously distinguished from the minjung and thus in his theology there is no such thing as what Bonino calls "messianic confusion."[36] According to his minjung messianism, the minjung have a messianic role, characteristic, or function in such a way that without receiving the minjung one cannot receive Jesus. The suffering and cry of the minjung function as the call of Christ for people to see the injustice and sinfulness of the world caused by the powerful and to turn away from such evil practice of the world by identifying with the poor minjung. It is like the call for the faith that proves itself with works. Thus, he asserts, "In order to accept the gospel of Jesus according to Scripture and thus to be saved, we must demonstrate solidarity with today's poor. There is no way to accept the gospel without standing in solidarity with the poor."[37] Lying behind the different understandings of minjung messianism between Suh and Ahn is a more fundamental difference between them with regard to the being and the work of Jesus.

Suh affirms the divinity of Jesus while Ahn categorically denies it. "There is a God," Suh says, "who came to the poor and the oppressed, and

---

34. Nam-dong Suh, "Envisagement of Han," 345.
35. Ibid.
36. Bonino, "Latin American Looks," 167.
37. Nam-dong Suh, *Study in Minjung Theology*, 405.

he is Jesus."³⁸ Reminiscent of the saying of Jesus in Mark 10:45, which reads, "For the Son of Man came not to be served but to serve, and to give his life a ransom for many," he contends that "the reason God came in human form is not to be served by humans but to serve them."³⁹ Criticizing the traditional Christian theology for merely talking about divine transcendence, Suh argues that the story of Jesus in minjung theology is the story of divine incarnation.⁴⁰ Based on these, Tae-soo Yim concludes that, in contrast to Ahn, Suh does not deny the traditional doctrine of the two natures of Christ formulated as *vere Deus et vere homo*.⁴¹

With regard to the death of Jesus, Suh gives primary attention to its sociopolitical implications, yet he still recognizes it as an atoning sacrifice for human beings. Jesus' death, according to him, is a *crucifixion*, which is an execution of a political criminal, but the church removed its political significance and changed it into the purely religious symbol of the *cross*. In this process, he argues, the redemptive event has lost its historical nucleus and the cross its power to transform history.⁴² Suh seeks to recover the historical and political significance of Jesus' death in his minjung theology but, nevertheless, he does not intend to simply replace the religious implications of the cross with its social and political ones. As discussed above, Ahn argues that the death of Jesus is a purely political event without any religious import. He rejects the religious significance of the cross as a distortion of the historical reality for the maintenance of the apostolic church authority. For him, the crucifixion inthe *kerygma* as a vicarious sacrifice is not compatible with the crucifixion in history as a political execution. Hence, he understands the passion narrative in separation from the *kerygma* and by rejecting the latter.

There is no such separation in Suh, however. As seen earlier, he suggests two ways of understanding the life and suffering of Jesus: one is a "traditional christological interpretation" in which Jesus' death is a vicarious atonement for human sin, and the other is a "pneumatological historical interpretation" in which the life of Jesus is to be imitated and the Jesus event to be recurred in the lives of those who work for the

38. Ibid., 13.
39. Ibid., 188.
40. Ibid., 299.
41. Yim, "Nam-dong Suh's Understanding," 116.
42. Nam-dong Suh, "Confluence," 247.

liberation of the minjung.⁴³ Of these two interpretations, Suh does not hold one over against the other but maintains that the two perspectives are not alternative, but supplementary, to each other.⁴⁴ This suggestion of Suh finds parallel in Moltmann, according to whom, as discussed earlier, both inclusive solidarity Christology and exclusive representative Christology should be maintained at the same time. Suh's minjung messianism, then, is not an attempt to replace orthodox Christology but to counterbalance it. In contrast to Ahn, who intends to replace the Christ of the *kerygma* with the historical Jesus as he understands him, Suh has no distinction between Christ and Jesus, and rather uses the words "Jesus," "Christ," and "the Lord" interchangeably.⁴⁵

So far in this chapter, we have discussed Suh's minjung messianism in contrast to that of Ahn, and now his answer to the first christological question we mentioned in the beginning of this chapter ("What kind of Messiah is Jesus?") is clear. For Suh, Jesus is the Messiah not only for the salvation of souls through his atonement of sin but also for the liberation of the minjung from all injustice and oppression. The transformation that Christ brings, according to him, is directed not only to the personal moral and religious aspect of life but also to the social and political arena. Promoting social justice and saving individual souls, he argues, are like the two foci of an ellipse and therefore should be considered equally essential goals of salvation; for him, if any one perspective is exclusively held it will lead to either other-worldly sectarianism or political fanaticism.⁴⁶ What is distinctive in Suh's articulation of minjung theology is his *both/and* approach in contrast to an *either/or* approach. While putting greater emphasis on the political significance of the crucifixion of Jesus, he still acknowledges the atoning nature of Jesus' death. Paying most attention to the fact that Jesus identified himself with the poor minjung, Suh nevertheless admits Jesus as the Divine incarnate. It is also in this way of the *both/and* approach that his thinking of the agent of salvation should be understood.

---

43. Nam-dong Suh, "Historical References," 177. Affirming the traditional christological interpretation, Suh writes, "Jesus of Nazareth has redeemed me from sin." In other place he contrasts the two ways of interpretation as "pneumatological-synchronic interpretation" and "christological-diachronic interpretation." See Nam-dong Suh, "Confluence," 272.

44. Ibid.

45. Yim, "Nam-dong Suh's Understanding," 118–21.

46. Nam-dong Suh, "Confluence," 250.

The Agent of Salvation

Suh is criticized as promoting a doctrine of self-salvation or "salvation from within."[47] Careful reading of his discussion, however, will show that this kind of criticism is rather one-sided and does not do justice to him. He contrasts the theology of "salvation from within" and the theology of "salvation from without" and criticizes the latter as fostering a magical religion.[48] His criticism of the theology of salvation from without, i.e., salvation by believing in the blood of Jesus, however, is not a denial of the atonement of Jesus itself but its abuse. What he rejects is the mechanical and incantatory understanding of the atonement of Jesus as unconditionally guaranteeing salvation to those who accept the doctrine. In this regard, he critically quotes the Rev. Yong Ki Cho, a well-known Korean preacher of the prosperity gospel. Cho contended, "Today many churches do not preach the blood of Jesus. Though they eloquently preach *the teachings and the life of Jesus* . . . they do not testify or praise *the blood of Jesus*."[49] According to Suh, however, merely preaching the blood of Jesus without paying attention to his teachings or calling for following the example of his life will be a way of a magical religion; for him, such religion "can be opium for the minjung but may not be a way of salvation for them."[50]

Unlike Ahn, who denies any divine redemptive providence in the death of Jesus on the cross, Suh affirms the redemption in Christ as bringing salvation to individual souls.[51] However, he vehemently criticizes the theology of salvation from without, in which salvation is considered secure by merely consenting to the doctrine of atonement without producing genuine change in life. In contrast, salvation from within, according to him, means regeneration of mind, heart, and behavior by the working of the Holy Spirit.[52] Contrary to common misunderstanding, it is not to advocate salvation by human effort without divine intervention. Rather, for Suh, it is the salvation initiated by the Holy Spirit, who works in the human heart to renew, change, and empower it. He denies it as a false idea that salvation from within is essentially connected with atheistic humanism. While salva-

---

47. Seyoon Kim, "Is 'Minjung Theology,'" 261.

48. Nam-dong Suh, "Confluence," 250.

49. Yong Ki Cho, *Salvation in Triple Measure*, 53; quoted in Nam-dong Suh, "Confluence," 250 (emphasis added by Suh).

50. Nam-dong Suh, "Confluence," 250.

51. Ahn, *Jesus of Galilee*, 259; Nam-dong Suh, *Theology at a Turning Point*, 103.

52. Nam-dong Suh, "Confluence," 250.

tion depends on human determination, Suh argues, such determination by human free will is in fact by the working of the Holy Spirit. So he contends, "It is because one has received the Holy Spirit that she can voluntarily make a decision of divine will as her own decision."[53] He calls this a salvation by divine-human cooperation or a salvation through *theonomy*, to borrow Paul Tillich's terminology.[54]

According to Tillich, autonomy, which is the natural law implanted in the human heart, and heteronomy, which is the divine law revealed from outside, were united in creation without any conflict. Due to humanity's fall, however, the unity was broken, and human reason can no longer fully comprehend divine will or properly align itself with it. Theonomy, then, is the reinstatement of the original unity of autonomy and heteronomy in redemption. In theonomy divine revelation does not exclude human reason, nor does human reason resist divine will.[55] Viewing from the perspective of theonomy, Suh understands that salvation is worked out by a human determination that is illuminated and empowered by the Spirit. Here the *both/and* approach of Suh in his understanding of the agent of salvation is clear. According to him, belief in the atonement of Jesus is not a magic spell for salvation but it should be actualized by a human determination in actively following him. Salvation is attained by faithfully following the cross of Jesus, which, however, is not merely a human choice but is wrought inwardly by the Spirit. For Suh, therefore, both the divine and human or, to put it another way, the atonement of Jesus and the following of Jesus, work together for human salvation.

According to our discussion so far, Suh's answer to the second christological question that was mentioned in the beginning of this chapter ("How does Christ bring about transformation?") is clear: he maintains that salvation is worked out by both divine initiative and human response. As our discussion of the first christological question (the scope of salvation) showed, Suh thinks of salvation in Christ as not only personal and spiritual transformation but also as social and political liberation from injustice and oppression. Such holistic transformation, according to him, is not achieved by human endeavors alone as if it all depended on human will and control, or by divine acts alone as if humans were only a passive recipient. He

---

53. Nam-dong Suh, *Study in Minjung Theology*, 165.

54. Nam-dong Suh, "Confluence," 250. According to Suh, divine-human cooperation is what Jesus and Paul teach about how salvation is worked out.

55. Tillich, *Systematic Theology*, 84–85, 94.

does not deny divine intervention in history, nor does he downplay human effort for salvation. Instead, he argues that salvation is realized by divine activity jointly working with faithful human response. What is unique in Suh's understanding of this divine-human cooperation for salvation is the messianic role of the minjung. As we have already discussed, Suh maintains that Christ comes in the guise of the suffering minjung to call attention to the fundamental sinfulness of the world, which is manifest in all injustice and oppression the minjung suffer from. To respond to the cry of the minjung by taking solidarity with them is to respond to the call of Christ in repentance and take part in salvation.[56] For Suh, therefore, the calling of Christ, who comes in the guise of the oppressed minjung, and the human response to the call in their solidarity with the minjung work together for salvation. Thus, the agent of transformation, according to Suh, is not just Christ calling in the minjung or those responding to the call, but both of them as they work in cooperation.

In summary, Suh's christological discussion is best understood in terms of the *both/and* approach. With regard to the christological question of what kind of Messiah Jesus is in terms of the scope of salvation he brings, Suh rejects interpreting Christ as only either a spiritual redeemer or a political liberator and instead holds that the salvation he brings is a transformation of both individual souls and society. With regard to the christological question of how Christ brings about transformation, Suh maintains that it is by both divine initiative and human responsibility that spiritual and social transformation is achieved. He sees Jesus as both the Messiah and the minjung; Jesus the Messiah comes in the guise of the suffering minjung and the minjung play a messianic role with their cry functioning as a call of Christ. With these christological understandings of Suh, we now turn to Richard Mouw's view of Christ and his redemption.

Richard Mouw's Christology: Cosmic Redeemer

We discussed Suh's christological understanding by focusing on two questions: what kind of Messiah is Jesus, and how does he bring about transformation? In this section, we deal with the same questions in examining Mouw's christological understanding to compare it with Suh's. Though

56. Nam-dong Suh, "Envisagement of Han," 344; Nam-dong Suh, *Study in Minjung Theology*, 180–82, 217.

Mouw has not developed a systematic Christology of his own but overall relies on orthodox Reformed Christology, two things are distinctive with his christological understanding that can be compared with Suh's. Mouw maintains that Christ is the cosmic redeemer with his redemption extending to all areas of creation, including social and political life, and that Christ implements his all-encompassing redemptive transformation in and through the redeemed people of God.

As with his view of the fundamental human problem, Mouw's christological understanding and its political implications can be best explained when we discuss it against the backdrop of the neo-Calvinist worldview. As seen earlier, the neo-Calvinist worldview renders the redemption in Christ as cosmic in nature, with its effect extending to all domains of human life and relationships. In this worldview, as Wolters succinctly puts, "[t]o conceive of either the fall or Christ's deliverance as encompassing less than the whole of creation is to compromise the biblical teaching of the radical nature of the fall and the cosmic scope of redemption."[57] Accordingly, in this redemptive vision there is no room for any two kingdoms thinking or a dualism between body and soul, sacred and secular, or spiritual and political. According to the neo-Calvinist worldview, redemption in Christ includes the transformation of everything distorted and misdirected in social, economic, and political life. In other words, the redemptive transformation not only leads to spiritual renewal but it should be embodied socially, economically, and politically. "Christ died," as William Dyrness neatly says in this regard, "not to make us angels, but to make us human."[58] While the neo-Calvinist worldview indisputably involves social transformation as part of the redemption in Christ and entails Christian commitment to it, it is Richard Mouw who has consistently applied this principle to the area of politics based on his understanding of Christ as the redeemer of all aspects of life.

The Scope of Redemption

No matter how inescapably the effects of sin have extended to all domains of human life, and no matter how deeply the distortions of the fall are built into the fabric of human relationships, for Mouw, this is not the end of the

---

57. Wolters, *Creation Regained*, 71.
58. Dyrness, *Earth Is God's*, 22.

story. "The God who had freely chosen to create," he puts, "now graciously decides to reclaim the lost."[59] In contrast to the two kingdoms advocates, he understands redemption in Christ not to be limited to the spiritual realm but to reach all areas of creational life. One of the rationales for this contention is his view of the all-encompassing nature of divine sovereignty and the lordship of Jesus. For him, it is Calvinist understanding of divine sovereignty that "God is not only sovereign over the processes of individual salvation . . . [but] he is also sovereign over the cultural patterns that have resulted from collective human activity."[60] Another rationale for this inclusive view is his holistic understanding of a human person. A human person, according to Mouw, is not only a spiritual being but also a physical, social, and political being at the same time in such a way that the fullness of salvation cannot be adequately experienced by those who are under social injustice and political oppression.[61] For him, the spiritual dimension of redemption cannot be effectively separated from its social dimension just as a human person cannot be successfully divided into spiritual and social beings.

While redemption in Christ is conceived of as influencing all patterns of human activities, including cultural, artistic, economic, and intellectual endeavors, Mouw's concern is specifically directed towards the political dimension of human interactions. For him, the biblical description of God's rule with the political term *kingdom* shows that the redemptive reign of God in Christ should be established in the political realm too, along with all other realms. The coming of Jesus into the world, according to him, was not only a challenge to the sinful distortions in personal and religious life but it was also "a threat to the political status quo."[62] In this regard, he is clearly opposed to VanDrunen, who argues that redemption in Christ applies only to the spiritual realm.

Two kingdoms Approach to Redemption

VanDrunen raises a strong opposition to the neo-Calvinist understanding of redemption that Christ's death and resurrection bring into the world. According to him, the redemptive work of Jesus is not to restore the original

59. Mouw, *Politics and the Biblical Drama*, 52–53.
60. Mouw, "Foreword," ix.
61. Mouw, *Political Evangelism*, 16–17.
62. Ibid., 24.

order of creation that has fallen but to bring a new creation that is a totally different order belonging to the world to come.[63] God will not redeem the social orders and institutes of this world, he argues, but the present world will be completely destroyed with the coming of the eschatological kingdom.[64] Maintaining that Christ's redemption is applied only to the souls of the redeemed people, VanDrunen makes consistent criticism against the neo-Calvinist idea of cultural redemption as misleading. For him, the only part of the current order of creation that will be redemptively transformed and accepted into the new creation, according to Scripture, is the earthly bodies of the redeemed people; in resurrection the earthly bodies will be transformed into spiritual bodies.[65] Based on this he argues, "Asserting that anything else in this world will be transformed and taken up into the world-to-come is speculation beyond Scripture."[66] Here we can detect the *either/or* approach in VanDrunen's thinking. For him, the redemptive benefits of Christ's work are applied only to the body and soul of the redeemed people and not to other parts of the creational order. Redemption in Christ and social justice, according to him, are mutually exclusive; redemption does not include restoring justice in the society, and achieving political justice has nothing to do with redemption in Christ but is only a matter of the present world, which has no value in the redemptive kingdom.[67]

In contrast, "the redemptive work of Christ" according to Mouw, "is, among other things, a *political* redemption," and the new life in Jesus is also "a new *political* life."[68] For him, it cannot be a feasible choice from a biblically informed perspective either to keep a distance from political involvement as if it has no bearing on Christian faith, or to give uncritical endorsement to political agendas. Instead, from the perspective of the neo-Calvinist worldview, he suggests seeing power dynamics and political relationships in terms of their createdness, fallenness, and being subject to redemption. If politics is also an object of redemption, then what does redeemed politics look like for him? To answer this question, we will need

---

63. VanDrunen, *Living in Two Kingdoms*, 62.

64. The New Testament teaching, according to VanDrunen, is that "the entirety of present cultural activities and products will be brought to a radical end, along with the natural order, at the second coming of Christ. Ibid., 67.

65. Ibid., 66.

66. Ibid.

67. Ibid., 194–95.

68. Mouw, *Political Evangelism*, 25 (italics original).

to consider how redemption is thought to work in the fallen creation in general and in the political area in particular.

The Redemption of Politics

While the scope of redemption is as big as that of creation, the life in redemption, precisely speaking, is not a *new* life but a *restored* life. As discussed earlier, in the neo-Calvinist worldview redemption in Christ is a restoration of the creational order that was enacted by God but has been disturbed by human disobedience. In this line of thinking, there is nothing that is intrinsically bad, as if it came into being independently of the creative power of God who is perfectly good. All creation is good in essence, and anything bad is accidental in a sense that it is a distortion of the original good. As Mouw spells out, political power as it is intended to be is part of good creation. It is to serve human communal life by properly distributing and exercising authority for making collective decisions and providing public services. Here divinely ordained authority is wielded within a proper limit and characterized by mutual accountability, responsibility, creativity, and servanthood.[69] The consequence of the fall, however, has distorted the ways political power is exercised so that coercion, manipulation, distrust, domination, and struggle may characterize it. Redemption of power, then, means a restoration of the fallen power to its responsible pattern.[70]

Another way to understand the distortion of the creational order in the fallen condition and its redemption is the distinction between *structure* and *direction* that Albert Wolters proposed and elaborated. By the term *structure* he refers to "the constant creational constitution of any [created] thing," which has its origin in the order of creation.[71] Every domain of creation has a structure of its own, and it is virtually equivalent to such philosophical terms as *substance* and *essence*. Even in a fallen state, the structure of a created reality cannot be entirely canceled out but still remains as good. *Direction*, on the other hand, denotes the two ways for a created reality to

---

69. According to Abraham Kuyper, every domain of created human life is given unique authority which is to be exerted within its own limited area and must not be violated by the authority of other domains. He calls this *sphere sovereignty*. For his discussion of sphere sovereignty, see Kuyper, "Sphere Sovereignty." For Mouw's discussion of sphere sovereignty, see Mouw, *Abraham Kuyper*, 23–27, 45–49.

70. Ibid., 45.

71. Wolters, *Creation Regained*, 49.

respond to the divine creational purpose for it. Whether it be individual soul, cultural activity or societal institution, it is always directed toward either conformity to or rebellion against the creational intention for it.[72] It is precisely in this sense that Mouw sees any human cultural endeavor not in terms of being good or bad in of itself but in terms of its being directed either toward or against God's creational design. So he says, "Under fallen conditions the question becomes one of cultural obedience versus cultural disobedience."[73] According to him, H. Richard Niebuhr understood this well when he succinctly observed:

> [Human] culture is all corrupted order rather than order for corruption . . . it is perverted good, not evil; or it is evil as perversion, and not as badness of being. The problem of culture is therefore the problem of its conversion, not of its replacement by a new creation; though the conversion is so radical that it amounts to a kind of new birth.[74]

For Mouw, political institutions and authorities themselves as creational structure should be distinguished from evil rulers or unjust political regimes that abuse authority in perverse ways. The former should be always recognized as having divine origin while the latter does not.[75] To use the distinction between structure and direction, the structure of politics can be described as orderliness in the authority-involved human relationships in the public arena, while direction can be either just ordering for common good or unjust and oppressive ordering for the interests of the ruling class. The impact of the fall on political life, then, is manifest in the directing of the political relationships toward abusive and exploitive ones against the divine intention for them.

72. Ibid.

73. Mouw, "Foreword," xiii–xiv.

74. Niebuhr, *Christ and Culture*, 194; quoted in Mouw, *Politics and the Biblical Drama*, 137–38 n. 15.

75. The early church father St. John Chrysostom already made this distinction and argued that not every individual ruler but the institution of governmental authority in itself was established by God. He said in his homily on the Letter to the Romans, "That every ruler is elected by God to the throne he occupies? No, this I do not say, answers the Apostle, I am not speaking about individual rulers, but about authority in itself. I mean to say that it is the will of God's wisdom that there should be authority, that some govern and others obey . . . Hence Paul is not saying, "There is no ruler that is not appointed by God"; rather, he is speaking of power itself and says, "There is no power that does not come from God: it is he that establishes all the powers that be on earth." John Chrysostom, "Homilies on Romans," 150.

Political redemption, then, can be understood as the restoration of the original direction toward just ordering in the political interactions that enables communal flourishing. Given the fact that the fall has misdirected the use of political authority in the oppressive and unjust way to the effect of victimization of the powerless and systemic corruption, political redemption must involve restoring the peaceful and just order for all, especially for the least of the society. According to Mouw, therefore, the redemptive project in political relationships must include both a ministry of compassion for the oppressed and a ministry of justice for corrupted political structures and practices.[76] In this regard, he believes that Christians have a twofold mission for the world: namely, "priestly" identification with the brokenness of the world before God and "prophetic" representation of God in his demand for justice before the world.[77] However, though distinctive from each other, the ministries of compassion and justice cannot be neatly separated.

Mouw sees serving the poor and seeking justice as being inseparably intertwined. For him, the Scriptures show so strong advocacy for the economically deprived that "a concern for the poor is a fundamental test of the faithfulness of the Christian community."[78] Christian concern for the poor, however, is not just an expression of generosity such as going the extra mile. It rather has its justification and motivation from the understanding of redemption in Christ. Mouw maintains that Christians must identify themselves with the powerless and share in their suffering "as [a] mode of participation in the redemptive ministry of Jesus Christ."[79] As a redemptive activity, then, the concern for the poor goes beyond personal goodwill or sympathy and requires a structural approach. For Mouw, the problem of poverty is not purely an economic matter but it is deeply related to the issue of justice, which reflects the impact of the fall on human structural life. Since "oppressive economic activity does not occur in a vacuum," but is done in the form of injustice towards the poor and oppressed, he argues that a political change to remedy injustice must be sought to help them.[80] In the redemptive approach to the problem of poverty, then, social justice as well as personal care and relief is crucial; not

---

76. Mouw, *Political Evangelism*, 15.
77. Mouw, *Politics and the Biblical Drama*, 68.
78. Ibid., 74.
79. Ibid.
80. Ibid., 80.

only compassion for the poor and oppressed but also passion for justice is key to political redemption in Christ.

Now, with regard to the first christological question ("What kind of Messiah is Jesus?") that was proposed at the opening of this chapter to set the stage for the comparison between Mouw and Suh, Mouw's answer is clear. For him, Christ is the cosmic redeemer whose redemption effects both spiritual and social renewal. Especially, he gives considerable attention to redemption in the political aspect of human life and, for him, political redemption is a transformation of oppressive and manipulative political relationships into responsible and just ones. With respect to the way redemption is brought to political life, Mouw focuses on the interplay between Christ's redemptive initiative and the responsible act of the redeemed people.

The Agent of Transformation

In Reformed theology in general and in the neo-Calvinist worldview in particular, God's work of redemption for the fallen creation is wrought by the death and resurrection of Jesus. In this tradition, therefore, it is without question that Jesus is the redeemer and the agent of transformation in a unique way. Mouw, however, maintains that God has prepared another agent for the transformation of the fallen reality in Christ. "God has chosen," he says, "to use a *people* as the means for expediting his redemptive purposes."[81] For him, the church as a redeemed people of God is called to be an instrument for redeeming the fallen world. In opposition to the view of the primary purpose of the church as fellowship of Christians "in retreat from the world," Mouw suggests to see the church as a task force with "an aggressive mission" for the world.[82] This mission, for him, is an essential one that makes the church be the church. So he contends, "[The church] cannot be the community God calls it to be unless it is also the agent of God's redemptive mission in the world."[83]

According to Mouw, the mission of the church as the agent of redemption is not limited to evangelism or spiritual renewal but includes renewal of the fallen creation. His view is clearly distinguished from that of VanDrunen. From the two kingdoms perspective, VanDrunen argues

81. Mouw, *Political Evangelism*, 24 (italics original).
82. Mouw, *Political Evangelism*, 38–41.
83. Mouw, *Politics and the Biblical Drama*, 81.

that the church is not supposed to do anything to advance Christ's kingdom on earth because, for him, Christ has already completed his kingdom by perfectly achieving God's creational commission that the first Adam failed in disobedience.[84] Interestingly, VanDrunen sees the disobedience of Adam not just as eating from the tree of the knowledge of good and evil against God's prohibitive command, but also as failing to keep God's cultural mandate of dominating the creation, including working and taking care of the garden of Eden.[85] According to him, though the first Adam failed to keep the cultural commission entrusted to him, which resulted in the human depravity, Christ as the second Adam fulfilled the task of the first Adam in perfect obedience and thereby brought the new creation. Thus, he writes, "Redemption is not about regaining the original creation but gaining the new creation by the work of Christ alone."[86] Here, VanDrunen shows his clear opposition to the neo-Calvinist understanding of redemption, which is typically expressed in Albert Wolters's work titled *Creation Regained*. For VanDrunen, Christian social engagement has nothing to do with redemption in Christ and therefore should not be understood as an attempt to restore the original order of creation by continuing the cultural commission rather in a redemptive manner. According to him, the cultural task originally given to Adam has been already accomplished by the work of Christ alone. Therefore, for him, Christians are not called as coworkers with Christ for the renewal of creation but are passive recipients of the new creation, which Christ alone achieves by his own work in preparation for the world to come.

VanDrunen makes a clear distinction between the present creation and the new creation and holds that redemption is a making of the new creation in the spiritual kingdom, which is worked out only by Christ. In contrast, Mouw maintains that redemption is a renewal of the creation. According to him, God has called the church to use as an instrument for the redemption of creation and this redemptive mission of the church is all-embracing. "In a world distorted by sin," he argues, "redeemed people must seek to bring all areas of human life into conformity with the Lord of creation."[87] For him, the church's mission as the agent of all-inclusive redemption is a natural corollary of the Calvinist conviction that Jesus claims all areas of life,

---

84. VanDrunen, *Living in Two Kingdoms*, 40–47, 51–62.
85. Ibid., 44–45.
86. Ibid., 36.
87. Mouw, "Foreword," x.

including cultural and political dimensions, as part of his kingdom. "To submit to the lordship of Jesus Christ," he says, "is to become committed to the political dimensions of his lordship."[88] Christian political discipleship is indispensable because verbal proclamation of the gospel and active participation in social service without altering the structures of the larger society are not enough to bring about genuine social transformation.[89] In this regard, Mouw argues that the Scriptures teach a "social gospel" of "the liberation of structures."[90] Nicholas Wolterstorff shares Mouw's conviction. The neo-Calvinist philosopher offers a perceptive statement for Christian commitment to social reform as a core of what he calls "world-formative Christianity." The following passage from his prestigious Kuyper Lecture clearly shows how the neo-Calvinist understanding of sin and redemption shapes their political vision:

> The structures of our social world are fallen. They are alienated from the will of God. Instead of providing authentic fulfillment to us who live within them, they spread misery and injustice, squelching the realization of what human life was meant to be. In response to this we are not to avert ourselves from our social condition, seeking closer union with God by means of undisturbed contemplation, for God himself is disturbed by our human condition; rather, we are to struggle to alter those structures and the dynamics behind them, so that the alienation is diminished and the realization advanced.[91]

For Mouw, any attempt to "alter those structures and the dynamics behind them" inevitably involves political activities. Christian political activities to redress injustice, then, are not a way of secularization to compromise the integrity of the evangelical truth, as some conservative Christians complain, but rather a sign of faithful witness to the cosmic lordship and redemption of Christ. Hence, in his *Political Evangelism* Mouw argues that political action should be considered an important aspect of the evangelistic witness of the church in such a way that it is as essential a task of the Christian mission as personal evangelism.[92] According to him, though error cannot be totally prevented from the church's practice and unanimity

---

88. Mouw, *Politics and the Biblical Drama*, 7.
89. Ibid., 70.
90. Mouw, *When the Kings Come*, 64.
91. Wolterstorff, *Until Justice and Peace*, 23.
92. Mouw, *Political Evangelism*, 7–8.

may not be possible for the church's decision-making, nevertheless, this should not keep the Christian from responsible involvement in political activity. He is not unaware of the danger lurking in Christian support of a particular political agenda or program. In fact, he is well aware of the temptation to equate political redemption in Christ with advocating a certain political ideology. Still, he maintains that the church should not shrink from making specific political choices or taking concrete actions. Political preaching and dialog in the church, on the one hand, can help the church grow in understanding the political dimension of the Christian discipleship. "There is no reason," Mouw says, ". . . why the institutional church ought not to sponsor political workshops and caucuses to deal even more concretely with political matters."[93] The church, on the other hand, must go beyond this toward concrete actions. There are times, according to him, when the church as an institute needs to take official stands with regard to specific political issues, whereas individual Christians can take part in political activities through "voting, holding public office, or participating in groups of Christians organized for action in area of politics, labor, etc."[94]

While political evangelism is an indispensable mission of the church for realizing God's redemptive purpose for the fallen creation, it is not aimed for a Christianization of society or an establishment of Christendom. For Mouw, "the most plausible political framework for Christians to advocate and support is that of a pluralistic society."[95] Political evangelism is different from the spiritual renewal of individual members of society; it is aimed at restoring justice and peace in human political relationships. In a pluralistic society, any one religion, including Christianity, cannot enjoy an exclusive privilege over other religions. Christian support of a pluralistic society, then, means Christians must seek religious freedom not only for themselves but also for those with other religious commitments and resist the temptation of using a coercive measure, even when it is available, to impose a Christian lifestyle on society in general. Thus Mouw maintains, "A concern to promote justice must be based on a desire that human beings be free to pursue the interests and projects that flow from their fundamental life commitments, *however regrettable those choices may be from a Christian point of view.*"[96] For him, political redemption is clearly

---

93. Ibid., 84.
94. Ibid.
95. Ibid., 95.
96. Mouw, *Politics and the Biblical Drama*, 79 (italics original).

distinguished from Christianization of the political arena; it addresses the sinful distortions permeated in the patterns of political practices and relationships but without attempting to impose religious values and patterns on the common life of society. In this regard, the distinction between the institutional church and the kingdom of God becomes necessary to the discussion of political redemption.

The institutional church, according to Mouw, is central to God's redemptive activity but is never to be identified with the kingdom of God, which must be bigger than the institutional church in scope. He makes a distinction between the church in a narrow sense, which is the church as an institute, and the church in a broad sense, which is the church as the Christian community. The former is "the people of God gathered for ceremonial worship and related activities," whereas the latter includes the former *and* other forms of Christian institutions and activities.[97] His distinction between the narrow and broad senses of the church corresponds with the distinction between the institutional church and the kingdom of God. The institutional church, he maintains, is "one among many manifestations of the kingdom of God" while the kingdom comprises of everything that submits to the lordship of Christ.[98] Accordingly, he sees institutions such as the Christian liberal arts college, the Fellowship of Christian Athletics, and the Christian family as the kingdom manifested in particular areas of life. For him, the Christian mission includes that but goes beyond the mission of the institutional church since "Christians are called to show forth the rule of Christ in all spheres of human activity."[99] The mission of the redeemed people of God as agents of redemptive transformation thus includes both personal evangelism and social transformation; and it is not oriented toward the Christianization of society but toward kingdom building in all areas of human life. This leads our discussion to the understanding of the kingdom of God as the goal of redemptive transformation, which will be dealt in the following chapter.

In summary, Mouw understands redemption in Christ as cosmic in the sense that it affects the totality of creation including, all aspects of human life and relationships. As discussed earlier, this amounts to his answer to the first christological question regarding the scope of the transformation Christ brings. For him, Jesus is the Lord not only of the spiritual

97. Ibid., 64.
98. Ibid.
99. Ibid.

kingdom but also of the civil kingdom as his redemptive project includes both spiritual and social renewals. Mouw, however, maintains that redemption in the political life should be distinguished from personal evangelization or Christianization of society; according to him, it is directed toward structural change to restore just social order and relationships. It is not personal evangelism but collective Christian social witness and activity through which the redemption in Jesus establishes the kingdom of God in the political realm. For this reason, Mouw regards the redeemed people of God as agents of redemptive transformation of the world. This, however, is not meant to compromise the unique role of Jesus as the redeemer of all created life. He rather maintains that, like redemption in all other areas of life, political redemption is worked out by divine-human cooperation in which divine redemptive initiative works together with the redeemed people's witness and obedience in the political dimension of life. This clearly sums up his answer to the second christological question we mentioned earlier regarding the agent of redemptive transformation. According to our discussion so far, Richard Mouw and Nam-dong Suh are comparable in their understandings of the scope of the transformation that Christ brings by his death and resurrection and how he carries out the transformation in relation with human agency.

Similarities and Differences

Richard Mouw's political theology is different from the thoughts of other Reformed theologians such as David VanDrunen in his understanding of the scope and the agent of redemption in Christ. Similarly, Nam-dong Suh shows a distinctive way of doing minjung theology. What distinguishes his minjung theology from the thoughts of other minjung theologians such as Byung-mu Ahn is how he conceives of the scope and the agent of the biblically informed liberation. In this section, therefore, based on our discussion so far regarding the two christological questions, we will compare Mouw and Suh in terms of how they conceive of the extent of the transformation that the Christian message should entail and the agent who carries out the transformation.

The Scope of Transformation

Our discussion in this chapter shows that Mouw and Suh are in agreement with each other that theology must be transformative and that the transformation is to be directed toward both spiritual and social dimensions of human life. One of the foundational statements of Mouw's political theology is that Christ's redemption reaches all areas of creation without exception. All political activities and relationships are thus subject to redemption from their sinful distortions and misdirectedness. According to Mouw, as the political aspect of human life is included in the divine plan of salvation, Christian witness and commitment to political transformation must be part of Christian mission. Promoting justice for the poor and the oppressed, therefore, is an essential part of Christian faithfulness to the gospel message. In this regard, Mouw argues that Christians must identify themselves with the oppressed in their concrete sufferings and, for him, this is to participate in the redemptive activity of Jesus Christ.[100]

There is a clear consensus between Mouw and Suh in this regard. For Suh, liberation from social and political oppression is essential to the salvation that the biblical message proclaims. Exclusion of the political dimension of life from the impact of the redemptive work of Jesus, he argues, is not the intent of the original message of the Gospels but its distortion in the process of spiritualization of the gospel message by the institutionalized church. In a similar vein, Mouw's political theology sets itself against the dualistic approach to redemption in Christ. Both Mouw and Suh reject the dualistic understanding of redemption regularly promoted by such theologians as David VanDrunen, according to which reality is divided into the spiritual and the social with Christ's redemption applied only to the former. Mouw and Suh agree with each other that redemption in Christ includes political transformation.

Further, they not only share their opposition to the dualism that depoliticizes redemption in Christ, but they also concur in their disapproval of the humanistic approach that despiritualizes the redemptive work of Jesus. Thus they are clearly distinguished from Byung-mu Ahn as well as from VanDrunen in their understanding of how far the scope of Christ's redemption extends. Ahn denies any spiritual meaning and influence of Jesus' ministry. In contrast, Suh, like Mouw, affirms Jesus' death as a vicarious atonement for humanity's sin. For them, the redemptive work of Jesus entails both spiritual

---

100. Mouw, *Politics and the Biblical Drama*, 74.

and social transformation. Their emphasis on political transformation as essential part of redemption in Christ, then, is not intended to deny or trivialize the personal and spiritual aspect of redemption but to counterbalance the much- and long-ignored aspect of redemption.

Based on our discussion so far, it is now clear that minjung theologians' accusation of Western theology as being dualistic and other-worldly cannot be fairly applied to Mouw. At the same time, criticism of minjung theology by some Reformed theologians as being materialistic and this-worldly does not do justice to Suh. As our observation shows, both Mouw and Suh maintain that the work of Christ for the salvation of the world is aimed not only for spiritual renewal but also for social and political transformation. They agree with each other that the scope of transformation initiated by Jesus' redemptive work encompasses both individual souls and social structures. They also share an affirmation of divine-human cooperation in carrying out the redemptive transformation.

The Agent of Transformation

One of the constituent features of Reformed theology is its emphasis on the sovereignty of God in his dealing with human history. From this point of view, some Reformed theologians have argued that minjung theology is an anthropocentric and atheistic theology. However, Nam-dong Suh shows a way in which minjung theology needs not deny the divine sovereignty in history. From the perspective of minjung theology, the Reformed doctrine of divine sovereignty is criticized as promoting political irresponsibility. Yet, Mouw shows a way in which divine sovereignty and human responsibility can be harmonized, and this is another place where his political theology and Suh's minjung theology show a close affinity with each other.

For Suh, it is not solely divine agency or merely human agency that carries out the redemptive transformation, but they work together in creative cooperation. According to his minjung messianism, one is saved by taking part in the suffering of the minjung. This, however, does not advocate a salvation through the minjung Messiah by human effort. According to Kyong-jae Kim, Suh maintains in his minjung messianism that the minjung play a messianic role in such a way that God incarnates in the minjung and works through them for his salvific plan. However, "the conservative orthodox theology," according to Kim, "does not understand [Suh's minjung messianism] at all while the humanistic or liberal theology easily misunderstands it."[101] For Suh, it is in fact Jesus the Messiah who comes in the guise of the oppressed minjung; to receive the minjung, therefore, is to receive Jesus and to participate in the divine providence of salvation.[102] Further, Suh contends that divine will does not invalidate human free will but can work in it through the Holy Spirit in such a way that a human being can voluntarily pursue a divine will as her own will.[103] He calls this "theonomy" and maintains that the divine will of salvation is accomplished by divine-human cooperation.[104]

Mouw shows a similar approach to the agent of salvation. For him, humans are not just passive recipients of the divine work of salvation. Human response in faithful obedience is an integral part of the redemption in Christ for both spiritual and structural renewal. For him, as God has chosen the human being as his partner for the ongoing work of creation, he has also chosen the Christian community as his partner for the redemption of creation in Christ. The essential task of the Christian church, therefore, is to function as "the agent of God's redemptive mission in the world" for both spiritual and social transformation.[105]

According to Mouw, the actualization of redemptive transformation requires Christians not only to witness the new life in Christ personally but also to live it out in all areas of life, including political relationships and activities. For him, God's sovereignty in history does not preclude the active role humans are to play. Especially, the *redeemed* people of God are the *redeeming* people of God for the whole creation in a sense that they are called to be the agent of God's redemptive activity in history. Thus, Mouw shows that the Reformed doctrine of divine sovereignty can be upheld without being socially irresponsible. He agrees with Suh in maintaining that God and human beings cooperate in the process of salvation in such a way that the divine action in Christ does not preclude human action in redressing what is fallen from the original state of shalom. There is, however, a difference between them with respect to the role of the church.

---

101. Kyong-jae Kim, "Seed of Grain," 213.

102. Nam-dong Suh, *Study in Minjung Theology*, 217; idem, "Envisagement of Han," 345.

103. Nam-dong Suh, *Study in Minjung Theology*, 165.

104. Nam-dong Suh, "Confluence," 250.

105. Mouw, *Politics and the Biblical Drama*, 81.

The Role of the Church

According to both Mouw and Suh, God works with human beings in effecting the redemptive transformation in Christ. With regard to how God works with people, however, they show a difference. Suh aligns himself with *Missio Dei* theology, in which mission is not seen merely as an activity of the church but primarily as an activity of God himself to heal and restore the world; thus the church itself is not the goal of mission but its instrument.[106] For him, God works in and through the Spirit without being limited by the traditional boundary of the church. Faith in Jesus, according to him, proves itself by following him in liberating actions for the oppressed minjung and thus taking part in the divine mission of salvation in history, rather than by merely consenting to the historical confessions of the church. To receive the minjung, he contends, is to receive Jesus and "without solidarity with the poor, there is no way to accept the Good News of Jesus." [107] In this line of thinking, God's liberating activity need not be mediated by the church or the Christian community and, consequently, the role of the church tends to receive less consideration. It is on this ground that Suh takes the Korean minjung tradition, along with the biblical and the historical church traditions, as a reference point for doing his theology. For him, commitment to the promotion of justice for the oppressed minjung need not be made in a specifically Christian way or as part of the mission of the church; any genuine response to the cry of the minjung, according to him, is a faithful response to the call of Christ and, therefore, will contribute to the mission of God to restore the fallen world.

Mouw, in contrast, develops his political theology within the boundary of traditional Reformed ecclesiology; for him, the church as the redeemed people of God is the center of the redemptive mission of God in Christ. Justice for the oppressed, according to him, is essential to the redemptive mission, but promoting social justice is not all about redemption in Christ. "Political and economic restructurings," he argues, "are important elements in the total kingdom picture, but they are not by themselves the total picture."[108] For him, non-Christian efforts for social justice should be ascribed to the divine common grace that is working outside of the church,

---

106. Nam-dong Suh, "Confluence," 239. For the understanding of *Missio Dei* theology, see Sundermeier, "Missio Dei Today"; Guder, ed. *Missional Church*; Bosch, *Transforming Mission*; Moltmann, *Church in the Power*.

107. Nam-dong Suh, *Study in Minjung Theology*, 405.

108. Mouw, *Politics and the Biblical Drama*, 73.

but it should be distinguished from the saving grace in Christ. Common grace, according to him, is God's favorable dealing with humankind regardless of having faith in Jesus. Unlike the special grace of salvation in Christ, "it is limited to temporal blessings such as God's restraining of sin that might otherwise destroy created reality, and impulses toward justice and efforts for the common good that are evident in the lives of the unredeemed."[109] According to Mouw, therefore, common grace can enable unredeemed people to seek justice for the poor and oppressed; however, no matter how genuine it may be, social justice is only part of the all-encompassing redemption in Christ and it cannot effect spiritual renewal. For this reason, he maintains that God has chosen his redeemed people to be the instrument for both spiritual and social transformation.

For Mouw, the church in a broad sense as the people of God is the agent of the transformation in Christ. In contrast, Suh maintains that God's redemptive mission goes beyond the boundary of the church.[110] Their difference is due to the fact that Mouw places more emphasis on Christian distinctiveness whereas Suh focuses more on the universalness of divine justice. No matter how clear it may be, their difference regarding the role of the church is more a matter of emphasis than an irreconcilable contradiction; Mouw's emphasis on the Christian community does not in principle rule out divine activity outside of it, and Suh's focus on the ubiquitous liberating activity of God does not necessarily deny the significance of the role the Christian community is to play for the liberation of the minjung. Their different emphasis can complement, instead of rebuffing, each other's perspective. The significance of the church in Mouw's theology can stimulate Suh's minjung theology to give more constructive attention to the distinctive role of the Christian community in carrying out a holistic transformation. Minjung theology, even as minjung theologians admit, lacks an adequate ecclesiology.[111] This has contributed to a thought among many theologians

---

109. Mouw, "Foreword," xv.

110. It is not clear in Suh how spiritual transformation is achieved in relation to the redemptive death of Jesus. It is in part due to the fact that his minjung theology is intentionally focused on the social and political liberation of the minjung. There are in fact several points that are not clearly explained in Suh's writings, which in turn have contributed to different interpretations of his theology. According to Yim, Suh's theological thought is not systematically organized and this may be due to his untimely death. Yim, "Nam-dong Suh's Understanding," 114.

111. According to a survey conducted by the Institute of Minjung Theology in 1993–1994, the lack of ecclesiology was identified as the most significant factor for the decline of minjung theology. See "Survey of the Minjung Churches," in IMT, *Is Minjung the Messiah?*, 200.

that minjung theology amounts to a mere social ideology because it denies the uniquenss of the Christian church. Mouw has upheld Christian active involvement for social transformation based on a Reformed ecclesiology. Grounded in a more coherent ecclesiology that clarifies the church's role in God's redemptive dealing with the world, Suh's minjung theology would be able to more persuasively inspire the Korean church to engage in a dedicated and enhanced ministry for the liberation of the minjung.

Suh's emphasis on the divine activity of liberation in the secular world, on the other hand, can challenge Mouw's Reformed theology to be more responsive to the suffering and struggle of the oppressed. It can also make Reformed transforming activities more appreciative of non-Christian endeavors for social justice and more open to collaboration with them. Social ethics based on the Reformed worldview tends to focus more on the Christian community as the agent of Christ's redemption and give less consideration to non-Christian activities for social transformation. Though Mouw is more approving to secular activities for social justice than other Reformed theologians are, his political theology is still church-centric. No matter how right it may be to emphasize the centrality of the church in Christ's redemptive activity, this emphasis has always shown a tendency to underrate divine activity outside the church. Suh's minjung theology can provide a necessary correction to this tendency. He puts a strong emphasis on the divine activity of justice and mercy in the secular world without ignoring the spiritual side of redemption in Christ.

This approach of his minjung theology not only escapes the Reformed criticism that minjung theology has no concern for spiritual transformation; it can also enhance Reformed social ethics. In fact, his approach can offer a very compelling challenge to Mouw's theology. Mouw gives only a limited consideration to divine liberating activity outside the church, and therefore his theology is not very effective for social transformation in a non-Christian culture where Christianity is in the minority. In such a society Christian engagement in social transformation needs to have careful collaboration with non-Christian endeavors for social justice and should be directed by a broader understanding of biblically inspired social transformation. By constructively adopting Suh's perspective, then, Mouw's political theology could give more positive consideration to social justice activities outside of the church and have a more effective influence on the Christians who seek for social transformation in non-Christian cultures, including Korean society.¹¹² In conclusion, the difference between Mouw and Suh regarding the role of the church does not affect what they have in common with respect to redemptive transformation in Christ but can reinforce each other's perspective.

The Both/And Approach

Suh and Mouw show an undeniable agreement with each other that redemption in Christ is aimed for both spiritual and social transformation and is to be worked out by cooperation between the divine initiative and human response. This agreement in their theological reflections of the work of Christ is grounded on the *both/and* way of thinking they have in common in contrast to the *either/or* thinking of Ahn and VanDrunen. For Ahn, Jesus is the minjung but not *the* Messiah. Ahn's minjung messianism and traditional orthodox Christology are so contradictory to each other that they are mutually exclusive. According to him, the crucifixion of Jesus is one of the many messianic events that keep happening to the minjung throughout history, and the agent of salvation, therefore, is not Jesus but the minjung. According to Suh, in contrast, Jesus is not only the minjung but also the Messiah in a unique sense as the Divine incarnate. Suh develops his minjung messianism in a way that does not reject traditional orthodox Christology but counterbalances it. For him, divine intervention in Christ and the Holy Spirit does not exclude human response, nor does the latter deny the former, in working out salvation; they work in cooperation.

Mouw's harmonizing *both/and* approach is contrasted to VanDrunen's *either/or* approach. VanDrunen, while holding many significant Reformed theological convictions in common with Mouw, nevertheless contends that Christ's redemption has no bearing in the human social existence and builds only the spiritual kingdom of Christ. For him, the redemption has been already completed by the work of Christ alone and therefore does not need Christian involvement or the church's mission for any redemptive purpose for the society. For Mouw, in contrast, the redemptive transformation in Christ is directed toward both human personal and social existence, and also human relationships with God and with fellow humans. Applying Christ's redemption to only either one of the two aspects, according to him, does not do justice to the integrity of the human person as both a spiritual

---

112. This point regarding the cultural limitation of the Reformed worldview theology will be revisited later in chapter 8.

and social being. With regard to the agent of transformation, Mouw takes an inclusive view of the divine and human cooperation.

The balanced and inclusive approach of the *both/and* thinking in Suh and Mouw allows their reflections of the transformation in Christ to be mutually acceptable. Even though they show a disagreement regarding the role of the church, their inclusive way of thinking can make this difference not contradictory but complementary. Suh's emphasis on the divine liberating activity in the world (the *Missio Dei* approach) need not deny God's special dealing with the church in carrying out his redemptive work in Christ. Mouw's focus on the church, the redeemed people of God, as a pivotal instrument for the redemption of the whole creation in Christ does not necessarily reject divine redemptive activity outside of the church. These two different focuses of Suh and Mouw can complement each other's perspective and thereby contribute to a more holistic and cogent understanding of the messianic transformation of the world.

Our discussion so far has shown that Mouw's political theology and Suh's minjung theology share significant affinities with each other in their approach to the problem of sin and the transformation in Christ. With this observation, we now turn to an eschatological comparison between them to see how they conceive of the final state of the transformation in Christ.

7

Eschatological Comparison: What Is the Kingdom of God?

Nam-dong Suh's Eschatology

IN THIS CHAPTER, WE discuss the eschatological visions of Nam-dong Suh's minjung theology and Richard Mouw's political theology to compare how they present the final goal of the transformation that the Christian message points toward. The eschatological comparison is essential in our study because it will show how Suh and Mouw conceive the kingdom of God, i.e., the consummation of redemption in Christ. One's idea of the kingdom of God as the ultimate goal of history can epitomize one's theology, especially in terms of how they understand the fallen state of human life and its transformation. Suh and Mouw show important agreements in their approach to the eschatological consummation in Christ. For both of them, the kingdom of God is not an angelic state with all humanness in social and material dimensions eliminated; nor is it a social and political utopia that a successful revolution could achieve within history. According to them, the kingdom of God has significant continuity, as well as discontinuity, with the existing reality. Their inclusive and balanced approach to the kingdom of God makes their eschatological visions mutually agreeable and this becomes clear when their perspectives are viewed in contrast to the exclusive approach of Ahn and VanDrunen. We now focus first on Suh's eschatological vision and discuss it against the backdrop of Byung-mu Ahn's view, which is a more generally shared view among minjung theologians. When discussed in comparison with Ahn, Suh's distinctive approach will become more evident and will be more effectively explicated.

ESCHATOLOGICAL COMPARISON: WHAT IS THE KINGDOM OF GOD?

Byung-mu Ahn's View of the Kingdom of God

If eschatology is concerned with a radical change in the present order of life, then one's eschatology cannot be separated from one's understanding of Jesus' resurrection. Byung-mu Ahn rejects the bodily resurrection of Jesus and attempts instead to explain his resurrection from a sociological perspective.[1] For him, Jesus' death is a political execution without any religious end and meaning but symbolizes the suffering and death of the minjung of his time. Also, the New Testament accounts of the resurrection of Jesus, according to him, are not a report of Jesus being raised from the dead but a symbolic description of the minjung's awakening and rising from the despair that had held them captive. Jesus' death, Ahn maintains, was not only a culmination of the minjung's miserable defeat and suffering, but it also served to strengthen them to rise in solidarity. He contends that the Greek verb ἐγείρω that is used in the New Testament to denote Jesus being resurrected from the dead (for example, in Mark 16:6) basically means "to rise" or "to rise in action," and thus can imply the minjung's rise against oppression and injustice.[2] Ahn interprets resurrection from a sociopolitical perspective without any consideration of religious significance and, naturally, he understands the kingdom of God only from a viewpoint of an eschatology within history.

For Ahn, the concept of the kingdom of God is purely political and, therefore, it is a distortion of the original sense to understand it as a religious or spiritual entity.[3] Discussing several Old Testament passages about the kingship of Yahweh, he holds that the foundational idea of the kingdom of God is divine sovereignty.[4] For him, the kingdom of God is where only God rules without allowing any human power to rule over other human beings. The coming of God's kingdom, then, is the end of human kingdoms where the powerful oppress the minjung. Jesus did not attempt to define the kingdom of God, according to Ahn, because it was self-evident to his hearers; it meant liberation from political oppression and economic exploitation by human rulers such as the Roman imperial power, the Herodian dynasty, and the Jewish religious authorities.[5] The

---

1. Ahn, *Discourse on Minjung Theology*, 331–46, idem, *Jesus of Galilee*, 273–85.
2. Ahn, *Jesus of Galilee*, 285.
3. Ahn, *Discourse on Minjung Theology*, 252; idem, Ahn, *Jesus of Galilee*, 109.
4. Ahn, *Jesus of Galilee*, 104–10.
5. Ahn, *Discourse on Minjung Theology*, 230–43. Ahn interprets the miracles performed by Jesus only from a sociopolitical perspective, and this also shows how he

minjung's aspiration for the kingdom of God or God's reign, then, is for liberation from the tyrannical rule of the powerful in a concrete social and historical situation. In this respect, Ahn contends that the idea of the kingdom of God as the minjung's aspiration for liberation cannot uniquely belong to the history of Israel only.[6]

In summary, Ahn understands the resurrection of Jesus as the rise of the minjung from a deadly fatalism and the kingdom of God as the society where the minjung are liberated from oppression and becomes the subject of history. For him, the eschaton is to be fulfilled within history by human solidarity and struggle for the liberation of the minjung. Nam-dong Suh shares some important ideas with Ahn in his understanding of the kingdom of God but shows significant differences from him.

Nam-dong Suh's View of Resurrection

Like Ahn, Suh affirms that the kingdom of God is not something radically removed from the social, political, and material aspects of human life in the present world. He also agrees with Ahn that the liberation of the minjung from all kinds of oppressive and unjust rule must be realized within history. Unlike Ahn, however, Suh does not ignore the transcendental aspects of the eschaton. Their difference in eschatology basically lies in their difference in understanding the resurrection of Jesus.

While focusing on the political implications of Jesus' resurrection, Suh still recognizes it as a bodily resurrection in a literal sense that actually occurred in a specific time and place. He affirms that Jesus' historical resurrection is the first fruit of the general, eschatological resurrection. Based on 1 Corinthians 15 and 1 Thessalonians 4, he acknowledges the traditional belief in the resurrection at the last day, when Jesus comes again with the voice of the archangel and with the trumpet call of God, and those who belong to Jesus will be raised from the dead to meet him.[7] What he criticizes, however, is the popular belief in a resurrection that is based on the notion of cheap grace or a resurrection without the cross. For him, resurrection is

---

understands the kingdom of God. For example, the evil spirits in the Gospel accounts, according to him, symbolize Roman imperial power, and Jesus' exorcism, which signifies the coming of the kingdom of God, then denotes expelling of the oppressive Roman power. See Ahn, *Jesus of Galilee*, 165–70.

6. Ahn, *Discourse on Minjung Theology*, 236.

7. Nam-dong Suh, *Study in Minjung Theology*, 319.

the resurrection of the ones who suffered and were killed because of their faith and struggle for justice and truth.[8]

With regard to the political implication of Jesus' resurrection, he corresponds with Ahn that the Greek words ἐγείρω and ἀνίστημι, which have a basic meaning of "to rise" and are used in the New Testament to denote resurrection, can also indicate the insurrection of the minjung.[9] He takes Mark 13:8; Acts 5:37; and Acts 21:38 as examples in which the Greek words are used to mean political uprising.[10] Yet, he does not limit the meaning of the words only to the social and political insurrection but recognizes that they convey several different meanings depending on the context. According to him, then, when used in the resurrection accounts of Jesus the words not only denote his bodily resurrection from the dead but they also imply the uprising of the minjung who are awakened by Jesus' resurrection.[11] As discussed above, Ahn denies the bodily resurrection of Jesus and interprets his resurrection only as to mean the minjung's uprising against oppressive and unjust rule. In contrast, Suh understands the resurrection accounts of Jesus in both literal and figurative senses. For him, Jesus rose from the dead in a physical sense and his resurrection awakened the minjung to rise up for their liberation. While Ahn equates Jesus' resurrection with the insurrection of the minjung, Suh takes the latter as an outcome of the former. The difference between Ahn and Suh in their understanding of resurrection, then, accounts for the difference in their views on the kingdom of God.

Nam-dong Suh's View of the Kingdom of God

The kingdom of God, according to Ahn, is to be realized only through political liberation within history and, therefore, there is no room in his thoughts for the kingdom of God beyond history. In contrast, Suh presents an integrated perspective in which both eschatology within history and eschatology beyond history are maintained in harmony. For him, the kingdom of God is not what political activities can simply achieve, nor is it something totally disconnected from human experiences in history. He contends that the message of the kingdom of God has lost its transforming power because it has lost its original political implications. The kingdom

8. Ibid., 318–19.
9. Ibid., 320–21.
10. Ibid., 321.
11. Ibid., 321–22.

of God, according to him, has two dimensions essentially: the kingdom of God for the ultimate, and the millennial kingdom for the penultimate. "While the Kingdom of God is a symbol for the heavenly and ultimate," he says, "the Millennial Kingdom is a symbol for the historical, earthly, and penultimate."[12] The kingdom of God, on the one hand, refers to the heavenly realm where individual souls enter after they die, and it signifies a realization of personal and complete transformation beyond history. The millennial kingdom, on the other hand, refers to the new age and the new society established in history through social transformation.[13]

Regarding the heavenly kingdom of God, Suh contends that the immortality of the soul must not be rejected as a merely pagan idea but should be kept as a biblical or at least a legitimately Christianized belief.[14] Regarding the millennial kingdom, he seems to subscribe to premillennialism although he does not specifically mention the term or provides any theological discussion of the different approaches to millennialism. At one point, however, he says, "We enter the Lord's kingdom, that is, the Millennial kingdom when we are resurrected from the dead at the Second Coming of Jesus."[15] For him, the resurrection is not a resuscitation, which happens within the present order of life, but a resurrection into a spiritual body in the new society of the new political order.[16] The two symbols, the heavenly kingdom of God and the millennial kingdom, then correspond to salvation in a personal and spiritual dimension and salvation in a social and political dimension, respectively, and Suh argues that the one should not be separated from the other.[17]

In the early church, according to Suh, these two dimensions together constituted the message of the kingdom of God. After Christianity became the state religion under the auspices of Constantine the Great, however, the clericalist church authority removed the motif of the millennial kingdom from the message of the kingdom of God in the process

---

12. Nam-dong Suh, "Confluence," 249. He seems to borrow the distinction of the ultimate and the penultimate from Bonhoeffer. According to Bonhoeffer, the ultimate is justification of the soul by grace through faith and the penultimate is everything else that constitutes human natural and moral life. See Bonhoeffer, *Dietrich Bonhoeffer Works*, 149–60.

13. Nam-dong Suh, *Study in Minjung Theology*, 192–93, 319–20.

14. Ibid., 193–94.

15. Nam-dong Suh, "Confluence," 250.

16. Nam-dong Suh, *Study in Minjung Theology*, 319–20.

17. Ibid., 191–92.

of depoliticization of the Christian faith.[18] For this reason, he contends, the vision of the messianic (millennial) kingdom should be restored as a concrete goal within history. For him, neither the vision of the millennial kingdom on earth nor that of the heavenly kingdom of God should replace the other. He criticizes such Christian tradition that rejected the millennial dimension of the kingdom to push back the reign of God to the heavenly realm beyond history. So he argues:

> I have insisted on restoring the symbol of the Millennium . . . as a *counterbalance* to that of the Kingdom of God. The symbol of the Millennium which secures social justice must be restored and must run parallel to the symbol of the Kingdom of God which secures the salvation of the individual. Otherwise, the symbol of the Kingdom of God is apt to promote an other-worldly faith, while the Millennium to bring about a form of fanaticism.[19]

Against the accusation of his theology as seriously biased toward radical social justice,[20] Suh presents his minjung theology as an effort to achieve a balance between personal salvation and social justice, between salvation within and beyond history. It is clear that Suh does not reject the transcendental dimension of the kingdom of God but attempts to restore the whole picture of the kingdom by reconnecting the eschatological kingdom with the kingdom in history. In this way, he also believes that personal salvation and social salvation should be harmonized as the two effects of the same faith.

What is distinctive in Suh's eschatological thinking is that he regards the resurrection of believers not as something that marks the end of history but as a historical event that signals the beginning of the millennial kingdom on earth.[21] For him, Jesus' resurrection that occurred in history is the "precursor and guarantee" for the bodily resurrection of believers in the inauguration of the millennial kingdom within history.[22] In his eschatological thinking, therefore, history and eschatology are not clearly separated from each other but are overlapping. Eschatological transformation of society, according to him, must occur in history and this conviction reflects his, as well as the minjung's, aspiration for the new, liberated society where the

18. Nam-dong Suh, "Historical References," 162–63.
19. Ibid., 163 (italics added).
20. For example, Hyoung-hyo Kim, "Regarding the Truth."
21. Nam-dong Suh, *Study in Minjung Theology*, 123.
22. Ibid., 123–24.

reign of God is restored and the minjung becomes the subject of history. The final goal of transformation as Suh conceives of, then, is twofold: it is a transformation that is earthly as well as heavenly, social as well as personal, and political as well as spiritual. Suh's eschatological vision corresponds with Mouw's at this point.

Richard Mouw's Eschatology

Mouw takes eschatology seriously. He takes it to have "an integral relationship" to all other theological thinking.[23] Discussions of creation, sin, or redemption, according to him, are incomplete without taking eschatological perspectives into account. Eschatology as he understands deals with restoration of creation, ultimate purge of sin, and a complete redemption of all things. Mouw, therefore, discusses politics not only from the perspectives of creational order, human fallenness, and redemption in Christ, but also from the perspective of eschatological consummation. Three topics are essential in his eschatological thinking with respect to our discussion: political activity in the end times, the relationship of history and the eschaton, and cultural triumphalism.

Political Activity and the Millennial Kingdom

While he does not argue for a particular type of millennialism, Mouw argues that millennialism need not repudiate Christian political activity. Post-millennialists suppose that the thousand years of Christ's reign referred in Revelation 20:6–7 will be the period immediately preceding the second coming of Christ, while amillennialists take the thousand years symbolically rather than literally as the period between the coming of the kingdom of God through Jesus' ministry and its completion in his return. In either view, according to Mouw, Christian political engagement can be justified as a witness to the reign of Christ.[24] Those who hold premillennialism to the extreme, however, are often pessimistic about Christian involvement in social transformation as they believe that little or no progress in social justice and peace will be possible until the millennial kingdom is miraculously inaugurated with the coming of Christ. Hence it is not un-

---

23. Mouw, *Politics and the Biblical Drama*, 117.
24. Mouw, *Political Evangelism*, 28.

usual, as Mouw observes, that Christians often hesitate or clearly refuse to engage in political activities to improve social conditions on the ground of their conviction that true justice and peace will not be available and poverty will not be removed until Jesus comes to put an end to human history and establish his eschatological kingdom.[25]

This must not be the only way to hold the premillennial view of the eschaton, according to Mouw. He approvingly quotes Vernon Grounds, a premillennialist, to argue that premillennialism does not necessarily renounce responsible Christian engagement in social and political activity as futile. According to Grounds, while the world will be fundamentally changed by divine intervention at the return of Jesus, "there is no biblical reason for concluding that enormous evils cannot be significantly changed before [Christ] comes back."[26] For him, the redemptive transformation need not wait until the coming of the millennial kingdom, but the church must work to bring about revolutionary changes in the present life. In line with him, Mouw contends that no matter how one may conceive of millennialism, a concern for the poor and oppressed should never stop at any moment being a faithful response to the divine mandate. Even when no meaningful degree of social and political transformation seems possible, he adds, Christians are still called to witness faithfully to the redemption in Christ, to which every dimension of created life is subject.[27] This may be called prophetic pessimism instead of world-negating pessimism.

The Old Testament prophets, Mouw observes, did not promote "passive futurism" but delivered God's message from the perspective of "a dialectic of fear and hope."[28] They were distressed over widespread idolatry, political corruption, and social injustice. No immediate remedy was being anticipated, and they had to proclaim the impending judgment of God. Their pessimism was, nevertheless, accompanied by the hope that justice and peace would triumph when God finally accomplishes his redemptive plan. With the mixed feeling of despair and hope, therefore, the prophets never gave up proclaiming boldly the message of both the demand of repentance and the hope of restoration. For Mouw, this is how the eschatological visions should bear on Christian social involvement. He writes, ". . . the church is equipped with prophetic visions in order to act responsibly *in*

---

25. Ibid.
26. Grounds, "Bombs or Bibles," 6; quoted in Mouw, *Political Evangelism*, 29.
27. Mouw, *Political Evangelism*, 29.
28. Mouw, *Politics and the Biblical Drama*, 122.

the present, in the confidence that God has promised the ultimate triumph of justice and righteousness."[29] According to him, therefore, a vision of eschatological consummation does not make one politically inactive or indifferent but encourages them to seek for justice and peace even in the hopelessly corrupt societies.

This political activism of Mouw grounded on the eschatological hope is different from VanDrunen's two kingdoms approach. VanDrunen recognizes the importance of political order as ordained by God for a peaceful, orderly, and flourishing life in this world.[30] He also admits that it is a Christian moral responsibility to engage in cultural activities in a manner befitting a servant of Christ. However, he emphasizes that political justice belongs to the realm of this world, which is provisional and passing, and therefore must not be construed as a means to contribute to the advancement of the redemptive kingdom.[31] In this way of thinking, Christian activity to promote justice, no matter how good a work it may be considered, is not a matter of the kingdom of Christ, which is of utmost importance to the Christians, and thus can be regarded as a nonessential, secondary task. In contrast, Mouw sees the Christian political activity to promote justice as having a redemptive character, which makes the activity to be considered part of the essential Christian mission. His affirmation of Christian political activity is also guided by his conviction that eschatological transformation does not replace the present orders of life with radically different ones, but restores them.

Continuity between History and Eschatology

According to Mouw, eschatology is not something that is completely separated from history, but there is continuity between them. His view is contrasted to that of VanDrunen, who denies any cultural continuity between this world and the world to come. VanDrunen rejects as unwarranted speculation the idea that cultural activities and institutes of this world can be transformed according to the pattern of the redemptive kingdom of Christ and be received into the eternal kingdom. For him, the only thing of this world that has continuity with the world to come and will be transformed to enter it is the earthly bodies of believers because their bodies will

---

29. Ibid., 121–22 (italics original).
30. VanDrunen, *Living in Two Kingdoms*, 194.
31. Ibid., 194–95, 204.

be transformed into resurrected bodies. So he says, "*Believers themselves are the point of continuity between this creation and the new creation.*"[32] Everything else that belongs to this creation, according to VanDrunen, will be brought to a catastrophic end. In contrast, Mouw argues for continuity between the current order of creation and the new order of eschatological kingdom. In this regard, he makes two arguments in terms of how the eschaton will deal with the cultural development in history on the one hand and injustice experienced in history on the other hand.

To begin with, eschatological consummation, according to him, is not meant to negate human historical and cultural developments on earth as something fundamentally unacceptable to the new heaven and the new earth. On the contrary, everything good, whether it be natural or cultural, will be received into the kingdom of God. In this regard, he contends that eschatological consummation will not simply destroy the old orders and human developments in cultural life, but will purify and transform them all to make them fitting for the life in the kingdom of God.[33] In his discussion of the eschatological vision in Revelation 21:22–27, Mouw focuses on the statement that the kings of the earth will bring their glory and honor into the New Jerusalem (vv. 24, 26). While reluctant to suggest a definite identity of the kings of the earth, he wants to find "the significant conceptual point" that the statement makes.[34] According to him, the kings of the earth signify political and cultural representatives, and bringing their glory and honor into the New Jerusalem means two things: the kingship of Christ will be officially and universally recognized, and all cultural riches developed in human history will be received into the kingdom of God.[35] Among such cultural developments are political institutional life and various creative activities in art and literature. They will enter the New Jerusalem as the curse from the humanity's fall will be removed from the political and cultural activities too.

32. Ibid., 66 (italics original).

33. This is a typical stance among neo-Calvinist thinkers. For example, Herman Bavinck, one of the pillar neo-Calvinist theologians, suggests that redemption "is never a second, brand-new creation but a re-creation of the existing world," and thus he writes, "All that is true, honorable, just, pure, pleasing, and commendable in the whole of creation, in heaven and on earth, is gathered up in the future city of God—renewed, re-created, boosted to its highest glory." Bavinck, *Reformed Dogmatics*, 4:717, 720; quoted in Kloosterman, "Response," 173–74 n. 27, 28.

34. Mouw, *Politics and the Biblical Drama*, 134.

35. Ibid., 135–36.

Mouw also discusses the eschatological vision of Isaiah 60 to contend that human achievements in cultural activities will not be abandoned but will be taken into the eschatological kingdom. He describes the New Jerusalem envisioned in Isaiah 60 as a "magnetic place" that draws cultural riches of the human society into it.[36] For this reason, according to him, "the contents of [the heavenly city] will be more akin to our present cultural patterns than as usually acknowledged in discussions of the afterlife."[37] With the cultural development brought into the kingdom, then, the eschatological consummation is not a simple return to the original state of creation but something greater than that. Life in the New Jerusalem will be the original creation *plus* human cultural development, which has been carried out throughout human history in accordance with the divine mandate to "fill the earth and subdue it" in Genesis 1:28.[38]

Inevitably and inextricably intertwined with the cultural development, however, are rebellious and idolatrous tendencies. In the eschatological kingdom, all idolatrous and prideful distortions attached to any cultural development will be removed, and all rebellious patterns of life which have caused oppression and poverty through unjust social and political relationships will be eliminated.[39] What will be received into the New Jerusalem, according to Mouw, is all cultural development added to creation *minus* sinful distortions.

Human history has produced not only cultural riches but also injustice recognizable in all dimensions of human relationship. For Mouw, eschatological consummation will not cancel out history but redress it. In the process of the final and complete transformation, there will be some kind of political settlement to remedy all injustice that has been experienced in history. Mouw sees that, in many cases, human vices arise from political life with political systems being directly and indirectly responsible for most of the evils.[40] Injustice produced by political systems, however, has gone unfixed and therefore he believes that there must be fair dealing with this in the eschaton. Thus he remarks:

> If we take seriously the idea that the New Age will be a time for the settling of accounts, we should certainly expect some kind

36. Mouw, *When the Kings Come*, xiv.
37. Ibid., 7.
38. Ibid., 16–17.
39. Ibid., 18–19.
40. Ibid., 23.

of political transactions to occur in the Holy City. And some Christians *have* viewed the Last Judgment in these terms. When Christian people have experienced political oppression, they have often longed for a day of political vindication. They have viewed God as a righteous judge who will someday set the political record straight.[41]

Politically conservative Christians, in contrast, tend to imagine the kingdom of God in apolitical terms. According to the vision of Isaiah as Mouw interprets it, however, those who *politicize* the eschaton are right.[42] Wicked rulers and governments have abused their power and authority in oppressive and exploitative ways, and there must be a political trial in the eschatological kingdom in which justice will be done publically for the evil rulers of history. So Mouw contends:

> Thus the sins that have been committed in political history will be publically exposed in the Holy City. God will not allow such wickedness to go unavenged. Political dictators will be led into the presence of those whom they have cast into prisons. Kings and queens will bow low before the widows and orphans whom they have oppressed. Cruel tyrants will hear the testimonies of those whom they have martyred. White racist politicians will wither under the gazes of black children.[43]

Eschatology will not merely replace history, nor will it simply throw into oblivion what occurred in history. According to Mouw, the wrongs of history will be made right in the eschaton. There is continuity between history and eschatology in a sense that the eschatological kingdom does not just transcend history but transforms it. In summary, Mouw contends that the kingdom of God will receive human cultural developments into it except rebellious distortions therein and remedy all injustice occurred in history. For him, however, the kingdom of God is in no way a human achievement. He is well aware of the danger of cultural triumphalism and in this regard he makes a clear distinction between history and the eschaton.

---

41. Ibid.
42. Ibid., 24.
43. Ibid., 33.

Against Cultural Triumphalism

Mouw's political theology, though focused on redemptive transformation in political activities and relationships in this world, is nevertheless guided by the hope of the consummation in the future beyond history. While the Christian church is called to faithful witness to redemption in Christ that transforms everything under the sinful distortion, complete transformation cannot be expected for within history. Borrowing the idea of Oscar Cullmann and others, Mouw understands the redemption of all creation in terms of "already" and "not yet"; for him, the rule of the kingdom of God has "already" begun in history, but its fullness has "not yet" come and should await the eschaton.[44] Accordingly, he views the redemptive transformation in history from the perspective of both its possibility and limitation.

Mouw recognizes the human depravity and perverse tendency to act selfishly even against the general rules of morality. He also observes that human rebellion has not just affected individual wills but "has *institutionalized* sin," making evil "a part of the very fabric of human sociality."[45] This makes it gravely difficult to achieve justice and peace in human social relationships. One need to be aware of these difficulties in pursuing social and political change and this attitude is generally called "being realistic." Mouw, however, understands being realistic in a different, and even opposite, way. For him, to be realistic is to see God's possibility rather than human impossibility. God's possibility despite human impossibility is revealed in the raising of Jesus from the dead by the power of God. From the perspective of resurrection, therefore, to be realistic is to take into account the transforming power of God that can incapacitate the most powerful evil. The disciples' despair and pessimism after the crucifixion of Jesus was proved "unrealistic" at the dawn of Easter and thus Mouw contends that "[t]he Christian community must live in the constant realization that what the world calls idealism is often God's realism."[46]

Political activism is an essential part of the Christian witness to the kingdom of God, and this is to be done in the conviction that political redemption is possible even if it may not be a complete one. According to Mouw, Christians should promote justice and peace in the world not only from the perspective of common grace that makes a partial peace and

---

44. Mouw, *Political Evangelism*, 98.
45. Mouw, *When the Kings Come*, 64.
46. Mouw, *Political Evangelism*, 92.

justice possible, but also from the perspective of redemption in Christ that enables genuine peace and justice.[47] A realistic approach to redemptive transformation in history, however, should recognize not only its possibility but also its limitation.

VanDrunen raises a concern regarding cultural triumphalism among some of neo-Calvinist thinkers, who, according to him, failed to understand the clear "distinction between the two kingdoms, between common and special grace, and between this age and the age to come."[48] Sharing the concern, Kloosterman understands triumphalism as "arising from an over-realized eschatology that sees [Christian] efforts as establishing and ushering in the kingdom of God."[49] Mouw is clear in his rejection of triumphalism according to which complete transformation is possible here and now depending on the faithfulness of Christian endeavor.[50] In triumphalism Christians are viewed as conquerors in their attempt at cultural transformation. Critical to such triumphalist attitude, Mouw argues that, despite the promise of final victory given in the resurrection of Jesus, Christian commitment to social transformation must not subscribe to a triumphalism that fails to see the Christian life as a cross-bearing in following Christ. "Christian political involvement," according to him, "must take place before the cross, and it must be a means of sharing in the agonies of the cross."[51] Everything under the distorting effect of human rebellion, including current political order, will be redeemed, but the full redemption cannot be attained before the divine intervention will put an end to human history. Until then, Christian efforts for political transformation will be a mixture of failure and success, and of despair and hope. This is why Mouw rejects the triumphalist approach to cultural transformation as unwarranted.

Mouw's refusal to triumphalism, however, differs from VanDrunen's. VanDrunen does not recognize the continuity between this world and the

---

47. Ibid., 98.

48. VanDrunen, "Kingship of Christ," 162.

49. Kloosterman, "Response," 173. Sharing VanDrunen's concern, Kloosterman, however, is equally critical of pessimistic inactivity "arising from an under-realized eschatology" that ignores Christian efforts for cultural transformation.

50. For Mouw, the kingdom of God is a gift from God at the end of history. So he takes seriously the biblical statements that the New Jerusalem comes "down out of heaven from God" (Rev 21:2) and that God is its "builder and maker" (Heb 11:10). See Mouw, *When the Kings Come*, 6.

51. Mouw, *Politics and the Biblical Drama*, 139.

world to come in terms of cultural patterns and activities. These are provisional and do not belong to God's redemptive project, according to him. Therefore, the eschatological coming of the kingdom of God will put a cataclysmic end to culture, history, and the world as we know them.[52] For VanDrunen, the Christian life is a cross-bearing pilgrimage on the land that is destined to pass away soon. Christians, according to him, are exiles or sojourners temporarily residing in a foreign land. "They are not like Israelites," he argues, "living in separation from the world in their own homeland but are like Abraham and like the Israelites in Babylon who lived in a land and participated in a culture to which they did not ultimately belong."[53] Christians are to live in holiness in this world in anticipation of the world to come and are not expected to transform the world, which has no eternal or essential value to them. From this perspective, a world-transforming Christianity is not only conceitedly triumphalist but it is also misleading.

In contrast, Mouw does not see why the pilgrimage image of the Christian life cannot be compatible with the Christian mission of cultural transformation. While dismissing triumphalism as an unwarrantedly optimistic view on political transformation here and now, he nevertheless upholds Christian political witness as part of God's redemptive project. According to him, although complete transformation will not be possible within history, still, history is a process of all-encompassing redemption in Christ. For this reason, Christians are called as agents of redemptive transformation in all areas of life, including political life, but at the same time they are warned that injustice and evil will not be fully overcome until the eschatological consummation. Christian political involvement, therefore, must be carried out as a mode of following the cross of Jesus with a willingness to suffer rather than expecting the glory of Christendom. Present Christian endeavors, however, are not vain efforts with an unsuccessful ending already anticipated but have a significant bearing on the eschatological consummation. Mouw thus contends that Christian political involvement must "be carried on in the *hope* that God will allow our present activities to count as preparatory signs of his coming kingdom."[54] For him, Christians in the world are not triumphal conquerors, nor are they mere suffering pilgrims, but they are suffering transformers.

---

52. VanDrunen, "Kingship of Christ," 163.
53. VanDrunen, *Living in Two Kingdoms*," 97.
54. Mouw, *Politics and the Biblical Drama*, 139.

What underlies Mouw's political theology is the vision of cultural transformation consistent with eschatological hope, which safeguards his theology from the temptation of both cultural triumphalism and otherworldly sectarianism. In this regard, Mouw's eschatological vision shows considerable affinity with Suh's though some difference in their emphasis should be noted.

Similarities and Differences

In their eschatological thinking, Mouw and Suh correspond with each other in many important points. Especially, they present similar views on millennialism, continuity between this age and the age to come, and the danger of cultural triumphalism, while their similarities are still accompanied by a difference in where they put their emphasis.

Millennialism and Political Justice

According to Suh, the original message of the kingdom of God has been depoliticized and falsely separated into two isolated symbols, the heavenly kingdom of God and the earthly millennial kingdom. Instead of emphasizing one to the neglect of the other, he calls for restoring the original import of the kingdom of God by reconnecting the kingdom in eschaton with the kingdom in history. While recognizing both dimensions of the kingdom, Suh focuses on the millennial kingdom in history as he thinks it has been long suppressed. The millennial kingdom, according to him, is a messianic kingdom of justice, peace, joy, service, and fellowship that will be established on earth upon Jesus' second coming.[55] Whole social, political, and economic relationships will be fundamentally changed to restore the justice that the minjung have long and painfully desired.

Mouw appreciates millennialism as rightly putting into expression the biblical vision of radical redemptive change that should someday occur publicly. "Millennialists," he writes, "have rightly insisted that it is not enough for Christ to rule in the hearts of the saints; his rule must be manifested in the transformation of political processes as we now know them."[56] He is not much into the theological controversies on millennialism and

---

55. Nam-dong Suh, *Study in Minjung Theology*, 319.
56. Mouw, *Politics and the Biblical Drama*, 135.

is rather agnostic about which prefix among pre-, pro-, and a- should be the right one for millennialism. While most convinced of amillennialism, however, Mouw takes the premillennial persuasion seriously and shows strong sympathy with it.[57] He is persuaded with the underlying conviction of premillennialism that a visible and concrete rule of Christ must be established in human society on a sweeping level. He says, "Will there ever be a highly visible display of the mighty being knocked from their thrones, the poor being exalted, the hungry being satisfied with good things, and the corrupt rich being sent empty away? Somehow, some way, we have to see it in the kind of world where we presently see the opposite happening."[58] Social and political justice must be done visibly and radically within history and, because of this conviction, Mouw contends that even those who are inclined toward amillennialism need to embrace that emphasis of the premillennial perspective.

In this regard, Mouw's view finds a parallel in Suh, who writes from the premillennial perspective. Both of them eagerly maintain that political transformation in its fullness must take place within history regardless of whether the period of a thousand year is literal or symbolic. In addition, though the millennium is supposed to begin with a divine intervention, they do not take it as a miracle in the future that justifies political inactivity and quietism among the Christians. Rather, they consider it a hope that encourages the Christians to willingly suffer in their struggle for the reign of justice and peace on earth. Their shared vision of political change in the renewed society also shows their shared conviction of continuity between the life in the present world and that of the eschatological kingdom.

Continuity

Mouw and Suh uphold the continuity between the cultural patterns and orders of this world and those of the kingdom of God. For both of them, the kingdom of God is not a totally new order but an order restored in accordance with its original purposes. Thus, the kingdom of God will be not only spiritual but also still social, material, and political in nature. In

---

57. Mouw, "What the Millennialists," para. 7. The amillennial view, according to him, "sees Revelation's millennial reference as a symbolic portrayal of the perfect Kingdom of Christ, established by his atoning work and, while presently hidden, will someday be fully realized in the new heavens and the new earth." See para. 6.

58. Mouw, "What the Millennialists," para. 9.

terms of the political relationships, what the kingdom will bring is not the end of politics but its renewal. According to Suh, the mode of the politics in the kingdom of God will be a service to others in such a way that those with political power must be a servant to all others.[59] Mouw also thinks that the politics in the kingdom of God will be a restoration of its original purpose from creation. So he resonates with Suh when he contends that in the kingdom "the patterns of political rule will be restored to their proper function of 'servanthood' in human affairs."[60] According to the vision of Isaiah, he maintains, "[k]ings will be transformed into nurturers and ministers" and "Peace itself will become an overseer, and Righteousness itself a taskmaster."[61] Instead of simply disappearing, therefore, politics will continue to exist in the kingdom of God but with rebellious and idolatrous distortions removed completely.

In contrast to those who consider the eschatological kingdom to be an entirely new creation, Mouw and Suh assert that in certain purified ways the patterns of the social and cultural life in this world will continue to constitute life in the eschatological kingdom. For them, this continuity is an essential reason for the Christian commitment to the transformation of culture and politics instead of renouncing them as this-worldly and transient. Both of them, however, are conscious of the danger involved in Christian cultural and political activity.

Against Triumphalism

Minjung theology is often characterized as an anthropocentric approach to the kingdom of God on earth.[62] Neo-Calvinist conviction is sometimes described as triumphalist in its approach to cultural transformation. Suh and Mouw are not only aware of such criticism against utopian or triumphalist optimism regarding social change, but, as discussed earlier, they themselves are also critical of unwarranted triumphalism. While vehemently promoting Christian political activity to advance justice and

---

59. Nam-dong Suh, *Study in Minjung Theology*, 402.
60. Mouw, *When the Kings Come*, 35.
61. Ibid., 37.
62. For example, Ucko, *People and the People of God*, 87. Noting messianic fervor with a strong utopian vision in minjung theology, Ucko argues that one may criticize minjung theology for its tendency to "völkisch" (glorifying the people). See also David Smith, *Theologies of the 21st Century*, 345.

peace, they are clear in recognizing that salvation in Christ cannot be reduced to political liberation.

They also reject the idea that human work without divine intervention can bring the kingdom of God on earth. Such fanaticism totally misses the reality of evil, which makes suffering and persecution unavoidable in the Christian commitment to redemptive transformation. Whether Mouw and Suh take amillennialism or premillennialism, there is no room for triumphalism in their thinking. From the amillennial perspective, the fullness of Christ's kingdom is hidden in history; from the premillennial perspective, it is not until the second coming of Christ that the fullness of messianic rule completely removes sinful distortions and injustice from all human relationships. They not only object to other-worldly apoliticalism, which ignores political implications of redemption in Christ but often proves to be a more active support of the political status quo, but they also reject political triumphalism, which fails to see the difference between "already" and "not yet."

As this discussion has shown, both Mouw and Suh take the political aspect of life as essential part of human social nature rather than as a temporal order only for the life in this world. They pay significant attention to the realization of social and political justice on earth without abandoning the hope for the eschatological kingdom. Here we can detect their *both/and* way of thinking, which allows them to maintain an inclusive and balanced view in their eschatological reflections. For them, political activism and eschatological hope do not exclude each other but complement and guard each other from the danger of both political freneticism of overrealized eschatology and political inactivity of underrealized eschatology. Regarding the relation between this world and the eschatological kingdom, they take a continuity approach in which cultural and political endeavors in this world are not negated in the eschaton but have significant bearing on the eschatological kingdom.

In their vision of the political transformation, Suh and Mouw keep a balance between the optimism of the eschatological consummation and the pessimism of the persistent evil in the present age. They hold at the same time the realism of Christ's reign already begun in history and the realism of the prevailing power of sin. The millennial kingdom perspective they hold in common also makes them keep a balance between passion for justice and an eschatological hope. This view of divine justice breaking into history makes them passionate about Christian witness to political transformation in anticipation of ultimate victory, but without falling into triumphalism. In conclusion, Mouw and Suh show significant agreements in the salient points of their eschatological thinking. Along with their similarities, however, there is a difference in their emphasis, which deserves our attention.

Difference in Focus

Mouw and Suh have a slightly different view of millennialism from each other. As we have seen above, Mouw is most persuaded of amillennialism while Suh takes a premillennial perspective. The types of millennialism, however, are not as much a problem with them as the political implications of millennialism itself. In their discussion of the millennialism, they show a substantial agreement in focusing on the political significance of the kingdom of God and its manifestation through the realization of social justice. A more important difference between them with regard to the eschatological thinking lies in their understanding of the relationship of work to salvation.

Mouw disapproves of faith without works as falling short of genuine Christian faith, but he does not think of works as a necessary condition for entering the kingdom of God. Suh, in contrast, seems to suggest that. For example, he emphatically rejects the idea that the rich can enter the kingdom of God. For him, without renouncing their possessions, and thus giving up being rich, the rich cannot benefit from the good news of Jesus. "It is an oxymoron like an expression of 'a round triangle,'" he argues, "that the rich can go to the heavenly kingdom."[63] He even asserts that if he were invited to the messianic banquet to which the rich and the oppressive rulers were also invited, then he would decline the invitation without hesitation.[64] He seems to suggest that one is justified or condemned by one's own work, which is clearly opposed to the Reformed theological conviction Mouw unswervingly holds to. Though enthusiastic about Christian commitment to social and political transformation, Mouw unambiguously affirms that one is justified by faith alone and that the kingdom of God comes by grace through divine initiative.[65]

---

63. Nam-dong Suh, *Study in Minjung Theology*, 195.
64. Ibid., 35.
65. Mouw, *When the Kings Come*, 6.

What Suh contends, however, does not necessarily contradict Mouw's view. Suh's expression should not translate into an endorsement of salvation by works. His emphasis on human responsibility is not intended to replace faith but to refute the popular belief about faith that promotes an other-worldly and socially indifferent way of life.[66] When he fervently upholds human moral accountability, it is not meant to ignore the significance of faith but to stimulate the understanding of genuine faith. His strong emphasis on the millennial kingdom, social justice, and human effort should be understood in terms of his intention to "counterbalance" the other-worldly faith that is immersed in the salvation of individual souls and is usually accompanied by social unconcern.[67]

Further, Suh discusses his minjung theology against the conservative and dogmatized theology that, according to him, has spiritualized and individualized Christian faith to the neglect of its political implications. He wants to liberate the importance of works in the Christian message of salvation from its captivity to a dogmatized *sola fide* theology and to reclaim a balanced view on faith and works. His strong emphasis on works should be understood in this regard. In contrast, Mouw generally has in mind those with the Reformed theological persuasion as his audience. He develops his political theology to convince them of the political implications of the Reformed theology, and he does this within the rubrics of the Reformed theology by proposing an integrated view of faith and works. In upholding a faith-producing-work perspective in a way relevant to the Reformed theological tradition, he does not need to set himself up against the Reformed theology by focusing on works over faith. Suh and Mouw have a different audience and a different emphasis from each other, and this must be taken into account to do justice to their arguments. The seeming differences in their understanding of the relationship between faith and works, and between human responsibility and divine initiative, are therefore due to a difference in emphasis rather than an antithesis between salvation by works and salvation by faith. Suh's emphasis on works does not deny the centrality of faith in the Christian message, nor does Mouw's subscription to the *sola fide* Reformed doctrine undermine the indispensability of works in salvation.

The *both/and* way of thinking that guides the theological reflections of Suh and Mouw can help understand their difference in a constructive way.

66. Nam-dong Suh, "Confluence," 249–50.
67. Nam-dong Suh, "Historical References," 163.

ESCHATOLOGICAL COMPARISON: WHAT IS THE KINGDOM OF GOD?

Instead of contradicting, their difference can complement and enhance each other's perspective. Suh's strong emphasis on human moral accountability can keep the Reformed understanding of faith from falling into a socially irrelevant and politically irresponsible one. No matter how legitimate it may be to put a strong accent on faith in the Christian message, since the Reformation it has too often trivialized the importance of the human moral responsibility. The danger of the *sola* in the Reformational motto of *sola fide* is lurking in all theologies in the Reformational tradition, and Mouw's Reformed theology is no exception. If the word *sola* is understood in an absolute and exclusive way, then the significance of human works is compromised and becomes incidental.[68] In this regard, Suh's emphasis on works can be an antidote to the misuse of the *sola fide* principle and can challenge Mouw's Reformed political theology to recognize more fully the significance of human responsible actions in the redemptive transformation.

Mouw's emphasis on the divine initiative, on the other hand, can also strenghen Suh's theology. There is a temptation of utopian humanism in every Christian endeavor to achieve social justice and peace here and now and Suh's theology is not immune to it. The more enthusiastic one is about accomplishing social transformation, the greater the temptation is. Suh's emphasis on works as a requirement for entering the kingdom of God can miss the divine grace and initiative in bringing about the kingdom of God. In this case, Mouw's Reformed view of the divine sovereignty in establishing the kingdom can strengthen Suh's theology by making his emphasis on human moral responsibility to be grounded on the hope and confidence from recognition of the divine initiative. In fact, without the divine initiative, Christian social action can lose direction and fall into utopian freneticism; without human responsible engagement, the divine redemptive project cannot be actualized in history. On this, both Mouw and Suh agree.

In conclusion, the eschatological visions of Mouw and Suh regarding the kingdom of God show considerable affinities with each other. They see the kingdom of God as both historical and eschatological reality with the political order radically renewed. Though passionate about social transformation, both of them reject cultural triumphalism as unrealistic freneticism. With respect to the qualification for the kingdom of God, they show different emphasis on faith or works, but instead of repudiating each other's point their

---

68. See Lochman, *Christ and Prometheus*, 31–33. See also Bonhoeffer, *Cost of Discipleship*, 43–46. For Bonhoeffer, faith without an obedient life of following Christ is a result of pursuing cheap grace, which is the deadly enemy of the church.

different emphasis can challenge and strengthen each other's views to achieve a more coherently integrated understanding of divine initiative and human responsible action for establishing the kingdom of God.

As we discussed so far, Mouw and Suh show significant agreements in their understanding of the theologically inspired vision of political transformation. What is rooted in their agreements is a *both/and* approach that they show in their theological reflection. Of the two contrasting ideas, they do not simply choose one over the other but attempt to harmonize them in seeking for an integrating perspective that is more effective for understanding theological problems. In this approach, two different views need not reject each other but can complement and strengthen each other. In the following chapter, we will review our discussions of Suh and Mouw in this study from the perspective of their *both/and* thinking. And before bringing our project to conclusion we will take a look at the two social movements of the Korean church during the 1970s and 1980s, which were inspired by the minjung theological perspective and the neo-Calvinist worldview, respectively. The comparison between these historical practices will facilitate our consideration of the compatibility between Mouw and Suh's political-theological perspectives both in theory and practice.

8

Crossroad of the Two Theologies

The *Both/And* Approach
of Mouw and Suh

MOUW AND SUH SHARE an inclusive and complementary way of thinking in their theological vision of political transformation. Concerning the human condition, they are in agreement that both spiritual alienation from God and social alienation in human relationships constitute the fundamental human problem that any adequate theology should deal with. Their approach is contrasted with one that is preoccupied exclusively with either the spiritual dimension of sin or its social manifestation. For them, human rebellion is manifest both in their relationship with God and in their relationship with fellow humans. Both impiety against God and injustice against humans are the roots of the human problem that need to be addressed inseparably. While focusing on social and political injustice, therefore, Mouw and Suh nevertheless do not ignore sin against God.

In relation to this, they understand salvation that Christ brings in terms of both the renewal of the individual souls and the transformation of society at the same time. According to Suh, social salvation and salvation of individual souls are not two separate goals of the Christian ministry but two sides of the same coin.[1] Mouw also maintains that the gospel of Jesus is not only good news of spiritual restoration but also a social gospel of structural renewal because redemption in Christ restores every aspect of human life that is under the distorting effects of sin.[2] Their approach is clearly distinguished from that of Ahn and VanDrunen, both of whom understand salvation in terms of *either* social *or* spiritual transformation only.

---

1. Nam-dong Suh, *Study in Minjung Theology*, 192.
2. Mouw, *When the Kings Come*, 64.

Mouw and Suh show the *both/and* way of thinking also in their christological and soteriological understanding. According to them, Jesus is both true God and true human, and the redemptive transformation is wrought by both divine initiative and human responsibility. In this perspective, divine sovereignty does not invalidate human responsibility, and human efforts do not rule out the divine governance of history. This holistic view is in direct contrast to the exclusivist tendency toward either pietistic fanaticism that ignores the Christian mission to social renewal or humanistic radicalism that undermines the divine activity in history. According to both Mouw and Suh, it is not solely by heteronomous working of God or by independent and autonomous working of humans that redemptive transformation is brought about; for them, it is through divine-human cooperation in which humans are called to participate in redemptive transformation in Christ and to carry out the transformation as an agent of divine redemptive activity.

Also in their eschatological thinking, Mouw and Suh take the *both/and* approach. Instead of advocating either the messianic kingdom on earth within history or the heavenly kingdom of God beyond history, they take both views as compatible visions of eschatological consummation.[3] Their approach is contrary to both the other-worldly perspective that takes the eschaton only as a matter of the ultimate renewal in the heavenly kingdom and the this-worldly perspective that confines the eschaton within history and thus mistakes the penultimate for the ultimate. Without falling into one extreme view over the other, Mouw and Suh hold that the reign of God will not only put an end to history as we know it, but it will also break into history, establishing the kingdom of God both on earth and in heaven. It is clear that, in the essential issues of their theologically informed visions of social transformation, both of them maintain the *both/and* approach. This explains the theological affinity the two theologians share in their sociopolitical ethics even though they work on different theological traditions from each other. This affinity between Mouw and Suh based on their *both/and* approach, then, can inspire a rapprochement between the minjung church movement and the neo-Calvinist worldview movement, which have been largely considered theologically irreconcilable.

---

3. Mouw, "Millennialists," paras. 9–12; Nam-dong Suh, *Study in Minjung Theology*, 193.

A Rapprochement between the Minjung Church Movement and the Neo-Calvinist Worldview Movement

As we saw earlier in chapters 2 and 3, the minjung church movement and the Christian worldview movement were Christian political involvements in recent Korean history that were prompted by minjung theology and the neo-Calvinist worldview, respectively. Despite their social and theological contributions, the two movements had limited influences in the Korean church and society and eventually began to decline in the early 1990s. In this section we will evaluate the two movements from the perspective of the *both/and* thinking of Mouw and Suh in an attempt to find out how their approaches can provide a way in which the two movements are reconciled for a more effective theological vision of political transformation.

Minjung Church Movement

The regime of the military dictators Junghee Park and Doohwan Chun in South Korea from 1961 to 1987 was marked by political oppression and economic exploitation. The Korean church at large was submissive to the oppressive power and unconcerned with political and economic injustice. While the minjung, the powerless in the society, were victimized, it was a time of rapid economic development for Korean society in general and explosive growth for the Korean church stimulated by prosperity theology. During that period, minjung theology provided a theological justification for taking part in the pro-democracy activities and standing in solidarity with the poor and oppressed for their liberation.[4] The minjung church became a voice in the wilderness calling for justice, human rights, and democracy in the name of the Christian gospel.[5] Small in number, the minjung church was light and salt in the dark period of Korean history.[6] Seyoon Kim, a trenchant critic of minjung theology, nevertheless admits that the concerns of minjung theology were not only relevant but also legitimate considering the

---

4. For a discussion of the development of minjung theology against the backdrop of the recent Korean history, see Küster, *Protestant Theology of Passion*, 19–26.

5. For a historical study of the minjung church movement, see Sang-si Jung, "New Prospect." For a theological discussion of the minjung church movement, see Ryoo, "Theological Review."

6. For reflections on the minjung church movement from minjung church ministers, activists, and lay people, see Presbyterian Church, ed., *Jesus Gone to Galilee*.

injustice and oppression inflicted by the tyrannical regimes of that time and the political indifference of most Korean churches that compromised the social teachings of the gospel.[7] He also appreciates the sacrifices, including imprisonment, made by several minjung theologians and the activists of the minjung church movement for the sake of justice and freedom for the minjung specifically and for the larger society in general.[8]

The contribution of the minjung church movement is not only practical in its protest against the unjust regime and its active solidarity with the poor and oppressed, but it is also theological. The vast majority of the Korean church was not only politically compromised by giving blind support to the status quo politics, but they were also compromising the Christian gospel by muting its social message. They understood salvation in both spiritual and materialistic senses; for them, salvation meant a deliverance of individual souls for the world to come and, at the same time, material and secular blessings for life in this world. Yet, they never thought of it in the social and political sense. Minjung theology challenged this individualistic understanding of salvation and called attention to a more holistic understanding of salvation that includes social and political redemption.[9] Though not popular among most Korean Christians, minjung theology and the minjung church movement nevertheless contributed to the broadening of the Korean church's understanding of salvation and the kingdom of God. Undeniably, it was in part due to the challenge of minjung theology that the Korean church began to recognize the social and political involvement as a Christian witness.[10]

Despite their valid concerns and challenges, however, minjung theology and the minjung church movement faced serious criticism from the mainstream Korean church. It was not merely a political reaction from the majority Korean church that was politically conservative; minjung theology itself was considered seriously unbalanced in its theologizing. It was not an

---

7. Seyoon Kim, "Is 'Minjung Theology,'" 258–60.

8. For a detailed description of the resistance activities of the Minjung theologians during the military dictatorship in the 1970s and 1980s, see Shin et al., "South Korea's Democracy Movement," 33–39. For an extensive historical study on the Korean Christian human rights movement in the 1970s, see Jin-bae Kim, *Democracy Movement*.

9. Eunsoo Kim, "Minjung Theology in Korea," 62.

10. The two important influences beside minjung theology that stimulated Christian social responsibility among Korean Christians are the social teachings of the Lausanne Movement and the neo-Calvinist worldview. For the history and theology of the Lausanne Movement, see Stott, ed., *Making Christ Known*.

unfair criticism that minjung theology was right in emphasizing the much-neglected social and political dimensions of the gospel but was wrong in doing so only at the expense of the spiritual dimension of the gospel. Minjung theologians tend to understand salvation only as an economic and political liberation and the kingdom of God only in its historical dimension.[11] If conservative theology understood salvation only in terms of spiritual renewal, minjung theology understood it only in terms of social and political liberation; they were critical to each other, yet equally reductionistic. Thus, not only the fundamentalist other-worldly theology but minjung theology also failed to provide a holistic understanding of the gospel, which must address both individual and social dimensions of salvation and both spiritual and political dimensions of the kingdom of God.

Another way of seeing the problem of reductionism in minjung theology is to examine its underlying anthropological assumptions. While the conservative theology tends to see the significance of the human being as lying in their soul and thus focus on saving individual souls, minjung theology regards them largely in terms of their social, economic, and political needs and overlooks their spiritual need and desire. This may explain why, as some critics of minjung theology point out, many of the minjung found comfort, inspiration, and empowerment in conservative or charismatic churches instead of in the minjung church.[12] In fact, the minjung church seems to have failed to win the heart of the minjung in general.[13] It is said that the minjung church loved and tried to win love from the minjung, but what minjung loved was the conservative church, whcih, according to minjung theologians, misled the minjung with false visions.

Many of the minjung in the 1970s and 1980s chose Rev. Yonggi Cho's prosperity theology and his megachurch instead of minjung theology and minjung churches. Despite the obvious lack of the concern for social justice and human rights for the minjung, Cho's theology and his church attracted numerous minjung. What is more, many of those minjung who came to Cho's church drawn by his famous message of the threefold blessing (i.e.,

---

11. For example, beside Byung-mu Ahn, whom we discussed in the earlier chapters, Yong-bock Kim contends that the culmination of God's salvation is the deliverance from all political oppressions and the establishment of a free and just society for the people. Yong-bock Kim, *Messiah and Minjung*, 8–9.

12. For example, see Seyoon Kim, "Is 'Minjung Theology,'" 262–63.

13. Interestingly, Byung-mu Ahn once stated that the success or failure of the minjung church movement will probably serve as judgment of minjung theology. Ahn, "Minjung Theology," 139.

a combination of spiritual well-being, physical health, and prosperous life) did experience self-transcendence and liberation from poverty and other miseries of life. Thus Seyoon Kim asks, "[W]hat right does . . . minjung theologians have to tell [the minjung] that they are mistaken or duped and stand in need of the proper guidance of the minjung theologians?"[14]

Despite its valid concerns and some significant contributions it made, minjung theology was not well received even by the minjung in general because it fell short of the holistic approach to salvation that is both socially and spiritually relevant.[15] Consequently, the minjung church movement began to lose its driving force in the mid-1990s, and this came in no surprise for many. In this regard, our discussion of Nam-dong Suh's exposition of minjung theology in the current study shows that a more persuasive way of doing minjung theology is possible.

Christian Worldview Movement

The neo-Calvinist worldview discussion was introduced to Korean Christians in the early 1980s. As we saw in chapter 3 of this study, the Christian worldview discussion provided a theological ground of Christian social involvement for evangelical Christians and triggered a social and political transforming activity, which is called the Christian worldview movement.[16] The Korean churches in the 1970s and 1980s were dominantly conservative in their doctrinal affirmations in general and in their belief in the authority of the Scriptures in particular. The neo-Calvinist worldview was able to provide a vision of social transformation that could convince a wide range of Korean Christians because the vision was solidly grounded in the biblical doctrines of God's creation, the human fall, and redemption in Christ. It reshaped the mind of those who had never been able to side themselves either with the accommodationist conservatism of their churches or with the activism of the minjung church movement based on liberal theology;

---

14. Seyoon Kim, "Is 'Minjung Theology,'" 262.

15. In this regard, Hyun-soo Kim, a minjung church minister, argues that the minjung church movement should keep the balance between the characteristics of being a church and the characteristics of being a movement. Hyun-soo Kim, "Church Characteristics".

16. For a historical survey of the Christian worldview movement in the 1980s, see Hun-soo Kim, "Retrospective Essay," 190–99.

the Christian worldview provided them with a compelling alternative to those two extreme views that were impractical for them.[17]

The Christian worldview motivated evangelical Christians to engage in social transformation activities in solidarity with the urban poor and laborers, as we observed earlier. Despite its potential as a compelling Christian vision of social transformation, however, the Christian worldview was not successful in mobilizing Korean Christians for an effective social transformation movement. First of all, it was because the Christian worldview movement was largely an intellectual movement. As generally observed, the Christian worldview movement began as a literature movement; i.e., proliferating publication of Christian worldview books in the 1980s, most of which were translations from Western sources, triggered the movement.[18] Those who played key roles in the worldview movement were Christian graduate students and scholars, and the worldview was "studied" through lectures, seminars, and study groups. A danger lurking in this approach is that the goal of the worldview "study" can be conceived in terms of understanding rather than doing. Thus, one could be satisfied with studying the worldview as a tool for interpreting the world rather than life-changing learning that leads to one's commitment to transforming praxis. In this regard, Jong-cheol Lee argues that a Christian worldview is useless if it cannot stimulate passionate involvement in social justice activities for the oppressed.[19]

Another problem related to this is an inadequate understanding of the worldview.[20] Although the central idea of the Christian worldview was the restoration of the whole creation in Christ, the dualist bias still hindered its proper appreciation.[21] Many of those who eagerly adopted the Christian worldview still maintained the dualistic understanding of the spiritual and

---

17. Jik-han Koh, one of the leading figures of the Christian worldview movement, observed the two extreme modes of faith among Korean young Christians as the personal spirituality focused and the social engagement focused and calls for a creative combination of the two concerns. Koh, "Personal Spirituality."

18. See Jong-cheol Lee, "From the Christian Worldview Movement," 126–27.

19. Ibid., 131.

20. Jung-gyu Cho argues that Confucianism, Buddhism, and shamanism all together have influenced the formation of the dominant Korean mentality and that this syncretistic religiosity kept many Korean Christians from adequately understanding the Christian worldview and made them conveniently use the Christian worldview only as part of their worldview. Jung-gyu Cho, "Korean Mentality."

21. See Hun-soo Kim, "Retrospective Essay," 200–203.

the secular, evangelism and social involvement, and the church and the world, putting priority always on the former and thus regarding the latter only as of secondary importance. The Christian worldview does not allow dualism that unnecessarily separates the one created reality into two because the worldview takes reality in its totality as subject to redemption in Christ. Therefore, according to the Christian worldview, redemptive transformation not only leads to spiritual renewal but it should be embodied socially, economically, and politically. The worldview movement, however, did not persuasively show that social transformation is not about going extra miles but doing what is essential as part of the redemption in Christ.

The Christian worldview is not just a call to putting into practice the fundamental beliefs of the conservative churches that are in principle authentic. It rather challenges the fundamentalist understanding of redemption in Christ, which has denied the public squares as the object of Christ's redemptive activity. The Christian worldview movement did not pay sufficient attention to this theological inadequacy and thus failed to stimulate the transforming social engagement as an essential Christian mission derived from the Christian gospel itself.[22] The Christian worldview, properly understood, is about orthopraxis prompted by the renewing of orthodoxy. The Christian worldview movement, however, did not successfully manifest the redemptive significance of social transformation and, as one minjung theologian suggests, this may explain some of the factors in why the Christian worldview movement caused little impact on the conservative Korean churches as a whole.[23]

Individualism and lack of proper ecclesiology must be noted as another reason for the decline of the Christian worldview movement. The Christian worldview usually gives an impression that individual Christians, rather than the church as a community, are the agents of transformation.[24]

---

22. According to Cheol-ho Han, the Korean evangelical student movement in the 1980s and 1990s prompted by the Christian worldview was not effective in making a transforming influence on society and, rather, was largely influenced by the situations of the surrounding church and society. Han, "Questions to the Korean Evangelical Movement," 19–20. Han, however, did not pay attention to the theological problem existing in the way the Christian worldview is understood with respect to the holistic redemption in Christ.

23. Hyung-mook Choi, "Critical Remarks," paras. 9–14.

24. For Hyun-jin Kim, this is one of the reasons for why the Christin worldview movement has been unable to make meaningful change in the society. According to him, the kingdom of God is the goal of the Christian worldview movement and can be realized by the church as a communion of saints, rather than by individual Christians.

Each Christian is called to work for the redemption in Christ to be effected in all areas of their life. Undeniably, Christians should bring their faith into all spheres and relationships in their lives, including the public square. Yet, the Christian church as a body of believers provides a significant dimension to the Christian witness. Since Christians are both individuals and members of the church, their witness and practice must be both individual and collective. It is not about a mission strategy but about the nature of the Christian church. As Christians are one body, the transforming social involvement must be an activity not only of individual Christians but also of the church, the body of Christ. In addition, considering the structural dimension of evil, the collective witness and praxis of the church is vital for the social transformation.

The Christian worldview movement, however, was not successful in promoting the church's collective praxis for social and political justice. It was in part due to the formulation of the Christian worldview itself. The Christian worldview was developed by writers from the Netherlands and North America, where democracy and human rights were relatively well established.[25] Particularly during the renaissance in the Christian worldview discussions of the 1980s, the mass movement for human rights and political justice was not an urgent issue for North American writers, while the Korean society was struggling with those issues.[26] The social and political context of the Western democratic society in which the Christian worldview was discussed prevented its writers from paying adequate attention to the collective praxis of the church against social injustice as a redemptive activity.

The Korean reception of the Christian worldview discussion was so enthusiastic that it was called a movement. However, the different social and political contexts between North America and South Korea were not

---

However, his emphasis of the church is limited to a life-sharing Christian fellowship like L'Abri. Hyun-jin Kim, "Church Community," paras. 61–64.

25. According to Hun-soo Kim, Koreans tend to understand the concept of worldview largely in a Western way of thinking because the concept was introduced through translations of Western writers' theoretical works. Kim, therefore, asserts that, in order to gain an appropriate understanding of the Christian worldview, Koreans need to have a deep understanding of their traditional way of thinking and a proper analysis of their social and cultural milieu. Hun-soo Kim, "Retrospective Essay," 207.

26. In this regard, Dae-young Ryu contends that the Western Christian worldview studies introduced to the Korean church in the 1980s had been developed in the political context of the Western civil society and therefore were not applicable to the Korean society that was under the violent military dictatorship. Ryu, "Theological Background," 72.

fully recognized, and this in part kept the Christian worldview movement in general from giving adequate attention to the significance of political transformation in Korea as a redemptive mission of the church.[27] Problems mentioned above, coupled with the prevalent theological and political conservativeness of the Korean church in general, have weakened the Christian worldview movement. In this regard, our current study shows that Mouw's political theology provides a more compelling justification for both individual and collective praxis for political transformation from the perspective of the Christian worldview.

Crossroad of the Two Visions

The *both/and* approach of Nam-dong Suh and Richard Mouw, as we discussed so far, can provide a more convincing way of doing minjung theology and the Christian worldview both in theory and practice. This, in turn, can suggest a possible way of reconciling the two theological visions for a more integrated and relevant vision of social transformation.

As pointed out earlier, the main problem of minjung theology that led to the decline of the minjung church movement was its one-sided understanding of salvation. While focusing on the social and political dimension of salvation, it failed to give legitimate attention to the spiritual side of liberation. The Christian worldview discussion, on the other hand, gave little attention to the significance of the collective praxis of the church with regard to the political dimension of all-encompassing redemption in Christ. This resulted from the dualistic tendency still hovering over the evangelical mind that subscribed to the Christian worldview. This led to the failure of the Christian worldview movement in giving adequate attention to political transformation.

The one-sided understanding of liberation in the minjung church movement can be remedied by the *both/and* thinking in Suh's presentation of minjung theology. While devoted to the liberation of the minjung especially from their social and political oppression, Suh nevertheless recognizes the essential significance of spiritual renewal. Unlike Byung-mu Ahn and other minjung theologians, he does not ignore the minjung's spiritual

---

27. Recent mass movements in Western society against neo-liberalism and economic inequality, such as Occupy Wall Street in 2011, call for theological reflections of the church and an updated understanding of the Christian worldview as a more relevant and viable vision of all-embracing redemptive transformation.

need and their aspiration for the heavenly kingdom of God. In this regard, Suh's holistic approach to minjung theology can be more convincing not only to the minjung but also to the Korean Christians in general.

The residual tendency of dualism in the Christian worldview movement can be corrected by the thorough application of the worldview principles to politics in Mouw's theology. While consistently adhering to the Reformed theological convictions in general, and the neo-Calvinist worldview in specific, Mouw upholds the redemptive significance of the Christian political involvement. For him, political orders and relationships are one of the most fundamental areas that are under the distorting effect of human fallenness and are in critical need of redemption. He also emphasizes the church's role and task in God's redemptive plan. The political involvement is not just a personal responsibility for some dedicated individual Christians; according to him, God called the church, the redeemed people of God, to be the agent of redemptive transformation in Christ. There is no room, therefore, for individualistic pietism in Mouw's political theology. For this reason, Mouw's holistic exposition of the Christian worldview can make the Christian worldview movement more relevant to the context of the Korean church and more consistent in its endeavor for political transformation.[28]

Further, our observation indicates that the minjung church movement and the Christian worldview movement need not necessarily reject each other. The theological affinities between Suh and Mouw that the current study have shown, and the holistic *both/and* approach that they share from the perspectives of minjung theology and the Christian worldview, respectively, suggest a possible way of reconciliation between the minjung church movement and the Christian worldview movement. In fact, there are growing conversations recently between the minjung camp and the worldview camp.[29] We cannot simply dismiss the theological and method-

28. In fact, considering the current slump of the Christian worldview movement, a number of evangelical Christian leaders try to find a way out of the impasse in terms not only of taking part in more active social engagement but also of rethinking the principles of the Christian worldview itself. Along with questioning if the worldview is too often understood as revisionist rather than as transforming, increasing attention is being paid to a more radical understanding of the worldview pertinent to the social and political situations of Korea. See, for example, Jung-hoon Jung, "Korean Evangelicalism," paras. 24–29.

29. For example, a minjung theologian was recently asked to write a critical essay on the Christian worldview movement to publish on an evangelical journal associated with that movement. See, Choi, "Critical Remarks," paras. 1–3. Jung-hoon Jung, editor of that

ological differences between the minjung church movement and the Christian worldview movement. Nevertheless, the theological affinities between Suh and Mouw provide the crossroad where minjung church movement and the Christian worldview movement can meet for a theologically more cogent and socially more relevant vision of transformation with renewed *theoria* and reinforced *praxis*.

---

same journal, who also wrote a critical reflection on the Christian worldview movement, was in turn invited to give a public lecture in a conference held by the Third Ear Christianity Institute, a research institute in the minjung theology camp. Jae-won Jung, "Model 1987 Evangelicalism," paras. 1–5.

9

Conclusion

Summary

REFORMED THEOLOGIANS AND MINJUNG theologians in Korea have been so critical to each other that there has been no constructive theological conversation between them. Reformed theologians such as Seyoon Kim and Eunsoo Kim were so harsh in their criticism of minjung theology that they counted it as a non-Christian or atheist theology. Minjung theologians were no less harsh in their criticism of Western traditional theology in general, including Reformed theology. According to them, traditional theology is not merely unsuccessful in fighting social injustice but it actually thwarts the minjung's aspiration for liberation by opiating them with an other-worldly interpretation of salvation and a spiritualized vision of the kingdom of God.

Reformed theological criticism, however, cannot be indiscriminatingly applied to Nam-dong Suh's exposition of minjung theology. Suh shows undeniable correspondences with Reformed theology in many essential points. Particularly, unlike other minjung theologians, he recognizes the spiritual dimension of salvation and the transcendental nature of the kingdom of God. Minjung theologians' accusation of traditional theology as a status quo theology, too, cannot be uncritically extended to Richard Mouw's Reformed political theology. According to him, human sinfulness lies not just in their spiritual confusion but also in every form of disorderliness in their social relationships. Therefore, the redemptive work of Christ, he contends, is operating both in spiritual dimensions of life and in all social and political relationships here and now.

Prompted by the holistic approach Suh and Mouw share, this study has been engaged in a theological comparison between them to find out how their theologies correspond with each other. It must be noted, however, that it was not the purpose of the current study to compare the minjung theology in general with the Reformed theology as a whole for any theological compatibility. From our discussion so far, it is clear that Byungmu Ahn's discussion of minjung theology is in direct opposition to the Reformed theology as VanDrunen conceives of. Suh's minjung theology, on the other hand, does not contradict Mouw's Reformed political ethics whereas his theology conflicts with the Reformed theology of VanDrunen. At the same time, Mouw's Reformed theology does not necessarily refute Suh's minjung theology despite some differences existing between them, whereas his theology is in sharp contradiction to Ahn's minjung theology. Mouw and Suh show significant agreements in their theological reflections, especially in their approach to political transformation. In contrast, Suh and Ahn betray fundamental differences in important theological matters despite the minjung theological conviction they share of the liberation for the minjung. Mouw and VanDrunen, too, disagree with each other in their understanding of political redemption in Christ, a central issue in social ethics, despite the overall Reformed convictions they share. To sum up, while there are irreconcilable differences between Ahn and VanDrunen in their discussion of minjung theology and Reformed theology, respectively, Suh and Mouw show considerable affinities to each other.

It must be also observed that, while our study is not a comparison between minjung theology and the Reformed theology in general, neither is it a general, far from exhaustive, comparison between Suh and Mouw's theologies in its entirety. As mentioned earlier, there are theological and methodological differences between Suh and Mouw, a detailed discussion of which is beyond the scope of our study. Our discussion has been focused on their theologically informed vision of social transformation and showed three major points in which they correspond with each other.

First, they are in agreement that what is fundamentally problematic in human life is their fall from the original state of life that God designed for them. This fallenness is manifest in the alienation they experience in their relationship both with God and with fellow humans, which reflects both spiritual and social dimensions of human brokenness. As a theological reflection of the essential human problem, their discussion mainly concerns the injustice deeply embedded in political relationships and social structures; nevertheless, they recognize the spiritual aspect of human fallenness as an essential part of the fundamental human problem, which any reasonable theological discussion of human liberation or redemption must address. For Suh and Mouw, therefore, both spiritual alienation and social injustice are the ultimate problem of humanity, from the dehumanizing power of which human beings should be liberated.

Second, according to Suh and Mouw, Jesus the Messiah is the agent of both spiritual and social transformation. For them, however, although the work of Christ is the foundation of the liberating or redemptive vision of social transformation, the divine scheme of renewing the human life is not carried out by supernatural intervention but works through human agency. While the work of Christ initiated spiritual and social transformation, humans are called to cooperate as an agent of redemptive transformation in Christ. Regarding the human response to the divine activity of salvation, Suh emphasizes the role of the minjung whereas Mouw emphasizes the role of the church as the redeemed people of God. Despite this difference, they concur in advocating human responsibility and the inward working of the Holy Spirit as essential elements of the divine plan for social transformation. For them, while Christ is the redeemer and the liberator, the liberation/redemption is worked out through divine-human cooperation.

Third, both Suh and Mouw maintain that transformation in Christ not only includes a social renewal in history but also goes beyond history. In contrast to those who take social transformation on earth as the ultimate goal or those who concern themselves only with spiritual transformation in heaven, Suh and Mouw take both the millennial kingdom on earth and the heavenly kingdom of God together as constituting the eschatological vision of the final consummation of social and spiritual transformation. This approach safeguards from both this-worldly reductionism of politically revolutionist theology and other-worldly reductionism of politically accommodationist theology. For both Suh and Mouw, the goal of transformation is not limited to the new society of justice and peace, but it extends to the all-embracing renewal of spiritual and social relationships in the ultimate kingdom of God.

In conclusion, Nam-dong Suh's formulation of minjung theology and Richard Mouw's neo-Calvinist political theology show significant affinities to each other in the salient points of their anthropological, christological, and eschatological thinking, which makes the two ideas compatible in their theologically informed visions of social transformation. This conclusion then implies a possibility of a reconciling perspective for the social transformation movement in Korea.

Theological and Practical Implications

For some critics, minjung theology with its movement and the Christian worldview with its movement have passed their heyday and are already outmoded. While blind repetition of the irrelevant theory and practice without critical reflections is a mistake, it would be equally a mistake to abandon minjung theology and the Christian worldview all together with their still valid claims and significant challenges both to the Korean churches and to the Korean society in general. Each of the two transforming visions has a legitimate emphasis on some essential aspects of the Christian understanding of salvation, but they failed to present a full and coherent vision of transformation for the Korean society. Each movement has distinctive strengths, as well as clear limitations, and this provides an opportunity for creative conversation to seek a theologically more coherent and socially more responsible vision of political transformation. The current study suggests that this vision can be developed from where Nam-dong Suh's formulation of minjung theology and Richard Mouw's neo-Calvinist political theology correspond with each other with regard to the social and political implications of salvation in Christ. A possible reformulation of the transforming vision, then, will uphold the liberation of the minjung as an indispensable aspect of all-encompassing redemptive transformation in Christ, which must include not only spiritual renewal but also liberation from social alienation, economic inequality, and political oppression.

Bibliography

Ahn, Byung-mu. *Discourse on Minjung Theology*. 2nd ed. Seoul: Korean Theological Study Institute, 1988.

———. *The Galilean Jesus*. Cheonahn: Korean Theological Study Institute, 1990.

———. *Jesus of Galilee*. Hong Kong: Christian Conference of Asia, 2004.

———. "Jesus and the Minjung in the Gospel of Mark." In *Minjung Theology: People as the Subjects of History*, edited by the Commission of Theological Concerns of the Christian Conference of Asia, 138–52. Maryknoll, NY: Orbis, 1983.

———. "Jesus and *Ochlos* in Mark." In *Minjung and Korean Theology*, edited by the Committee of Theological Study, KNCC, 86–103. Seoul: Korean Theological Study Institute, 1982.

———. "Minjung Theology of Yesterday and Today." In *A Review of the Contemporary Christian Theology for Pastors*, edited by the Presbyterian Church in the Republic of Korea, Ministry of Education, 127–42. Osan, South Korea: Hanshin University Press, 1992.

———. "A Reply to the Theological Commission of the Protestant Association for World Mission (*Evangelisches Missionswerk*)." In *An Emerging Theology in World Perspective: Commentary on Korean Minjung Theology*, edited by Jung Young Lee, 196–207. Mystic, CT: Twenty-Third, 1988.

———. "The Subject of History in Mark." In *Minjung and Korean Theology*, edited by the Committee of Theological Study, KNCC, 151–84. Seoul: Korean Theological Study Institute, 1982.

———. "The Transmitters of the Jesus-Event Tradition." In *Reading Minjung Theology in the Twenty-First Century: Selected Writings by Ahn Byung-Mu and Modern Critical Responses*, edited by Yung Suk Kim and Jin-Ho Kim, 27–48. Eugene, OR: Pickwick, 2013.

Augustine, Saint. *The City of God*. Translated by Marcus Dods. New York: Modern Library, 2000.

———. *The Confessions*. Translated by Maria Boulding. Hyde Park, NY: New City, 1997.

Barth, Karl. *The Theology of John Calvin*. Translated by Geoffrey W. Bromiley. Grand Rapids: Eerdmans, 1995.

Bavinck, Herman. *Reformed Dogmatics*. Edited by John Bolt. Translated by John Vriend. 4 vols. Grand Rapids: Baker Academic, 2008, 4.717, 4.720. Quoted in Nelson D. Kloosterman, "A Response to 'The Kingdom of God is Twofold': Natural Law and the Two Kingdoms in the Thought of Herman Bavinck by David VanDrunen," 173–74, n. 27, 28. *Calvin Theological Journal* 45, no. 1 (April 2010) 165–76.

BIBLIOGRAPHY

Beach, Waldo, and H. Richard Niebuhr, eds. *Christian Ethics: Sources of the Living Tradition*. New York: Ronald, 1955.

Bonhoeffer, Dietrich. *The Cost of Discipleship*. Translated by R. H. Fuller. New York: Simon & Schuster, 1995.

———. *Dietrich Bonhoeffer Works*. English edition by Clifford J. Green. Translated by Reinhard Krauss, Charles C. West, and Douglas W. Stott. Vol. 6, *Ethics*. Minneapolis: Fortress, 2009.

Bonino, Jose Miguez. "A Latin American Looks at Minjung Theology." In *An Emerging Theology in World Perspective: Commentary on Korean Minjung Theology*, edited by Jung Young Lee, 157–70. Mystic, CT: Twenty-Third, 1988.

Bosch, David J. *Transforming Mission: Paradigm Shifts in Theology of Mission*. Maryknoll, NY: Orbis, 1991.

Calvin, John. *The Comprehensive John Calvin Collection*. CD-ROM. Albany, OR: AGES Digital Library, 1998.

———. *Institutes of the Christian Religion*. Edited by John T. McNeill. Translated by Ford Lewis Battles. 2 vols. Philadelphia: Westminster, 1960.

Carus, William, ed. *Memoirs of the Life of the Rev. Charles Simeon*. New York: Rober Carter, 1847. Quoted in John R. W. Stott, *Balanced Christianity*, 11 n. 1. Expanded edition. Downers Grove, IL: InterVarsity, 2014.

Cho, Jung-gyu. "Korean Mentality." *The Christian University* 161 (June 1999) 10–11.

Choi, Hyung-mook. "Critical Remarks from the Ecumenical Camp to the Evangelical Camp." *Gospel and Context* 255 (January 2012). http://www.goscon.co.kr/news/articleView.html?idxno=28086.

———. "A Generational Approach to Minjung Theology and Various Minjung Theologies." *The Professors Times*, 19 April 2002. http://www.kyosu.net/news/articleView.html?idxno=2001.

———. "Several Issues in Minjung Theological Discussions of the 1990s." *The Era and Minjung Theology* 5 (1998) 345–69.

———. *Social Transformation Movement and Christian Theology*. Seoul: Nathan, 1992.

Chung, Paul S., Veli-Matti Karkkainen, and Kim Kyung-Jae, eds. *Asian Contextual Theology for the Third Millennium: Theology of Minjung in Fourth-Eye Formation*. Eugene, OR: Pickwick, 2007.

Clark, Gordon. *A Christian View of Men and Things*. Grand Rapids: Eerdmans, 1952. Quoted in Richard J. Mouw, *Politics and the Biblical Drama*, 32 n. 14. Grand Rapids: Eerdmans, 1976.

Commission of Theological Concerns of the Christian Conference of Asia, ed. *Minjung Theology: People as the Subjects of History*. Maryknoll, NY: Orbis, 1983.

Committee of Theological Study, KNCC, ed. *Minjung and Korean Theology*. Seoul: Korean Theological Study Institute, 1982.

Cone, James H. *Black Theology and Black Power*. New York: Harper & Row, 1969; Maryknoll, NY: Orbis, 1997.

Cooper, John W. "Church, Kingdom, and the Great Commission." *Calvin Theological Seminary Forum* 20/3 (Fall 2013) 3–5.

Dobbs, Lou. "Buffett: 'There Are Lots of Loose Nukes around the World.'" *CNN*, 10 May 005. http://edition.cnn.com/2005/US/05/10/buffett/index.html.

Dooyeweerd, Herman. *A New Critique of Theoretical Thought*. Translated by David H. Freeman, William S. Young, and H. De Jongste. 3 vols. Jordon Station, ON: Paideia, 1984.

———. *Roots of Western Culture: Pagan, Secular, and Christian Options*. Translated by John Kraay. Toronto: Wedge, 1979.
Dyrness, William A. *The Earth Is God's: A Theology of American Culture*. Maryknoll, NY: Orbis, 1997.
Frey, Bradshaw, William Ingram, Thomas McWhertor, and William David Romanowski. *All of Life Redeemed: Biblical Insight for Daily Obedience*. Jordon Station, ON: Paideia, 1983.
Goudzwaard, Bob. "Christian Social Thought in the Dutch Neo-Calvinist Tradition." In *Religion, Economics and Social Thought: Proceedings of an International Conference*, edited by Walter Block and Irving Hexham, 251–79. Vancouver: Fraser Institute, 1986.
Grounds, Vernon. "Bombs or Bibles? Get Ready for Revolution." *Christianity Today* 15 January 1971, 6. Quoted in Richard J. Mouw, *Political Evangelism*, 29. Grand Rapids: Eerdmans, 1973.
Guder, Darrell L., ed. *Missional Church: A Vision for the Sending of the Church in North America*. Grand Rapids: Eerdmans, 1998.
Gustafson, James M. "The Place of Scripture in Christian Ethics: A Methodological Study." *Interpretation* 24/4 (October 1970) 430–55.
———. "Preface: An Appreciative Interpretation." In *Christ and Culture*, by H. Richard Niebuhr, xxi–xxxv. New York: Harper & Row, 1951; San Francisco: HarperSanFrancisco, 2001.
———. *Protestant and Roman Catholic Ethics: Prospects for Rapprochement*. Chicago: University of Chicago Press, 1978.
Han, Cheol-ho. "Questions to the Korean Evangelical Movement." *Gospel and Context* 89 (May 1999) 16–23.
Hart, Carroll Guen. "The Doctrine of Creation: Judging Law and Transforming Vision: Response to Albert M. Wolters." In *An Ethos of Compassion and the Integrity of Creation*, edited by Brian J. Walsh, Hendrik Hart, and Robert E. VanderVennen, 57–61. Lanham, MD: University Press of America, 1995.
Hart, Hendrik. *Understanding Our World: An Integral Ontology*. Christian Studies Today. Lanham, MD: University Press of America, 1984.
Hart, Hendrik, Johan van der Hoeven, and Nicholas Wolterstorff, eds. *Rationality in the Calvinian Tradition*. Lanham, MD: University Press of America, 1983.
Hoffecker, W. Andrew, and Gary Scott Smith, eds. *Building a Christian Worldview*. vol. 1, *God, Man, and Knowledge*, vol. 2, *The Universe, Society, and Ethics*. Phillipsburg, NJ: Presbyterian and Reformed, 1986 and 1988.
Holmes, Arthur. *Contours of a World View*. Studies in a Christian World View. Grand Rapids: Eerdmans, 1983.
Institute of Minjung Theology, ed. *Is Minjung the Messiah?* Seoul: Hanwool, 1995.
John Chrysostom, Saint. "Homilies on the Letter to the Romans." In *Social Thought*, edited by Peter C. Phan, 150–51. Message of the Fathers of the Church. Wilmington, DE: Michael Glazier, 1984.
Jukjae Suh Nam Dong Commemorative Committee, ed. *Nam-dong Suh and Minjung Theology Today*. Seoul: Dongyeon, 2009.
Jung, Jae-won. "Model 1987 Evangelicalism Has Expired." *NewsNjoy*, 2 February 2012. http://www.newsnjoy.or.kr/news/articleView.html?idxno=36865.
Jung, Jung-hoon. "The Korean Evangelicalism: No Reform, No Future." *Gospel and Context* 255 (January 2012). http://www.goscon.co.kr/news/articleView.html?idxno=28083.

Jung, Kang-gil. *Whitehead and Reconstruction of Minjung Theology*. 2nd ed. Seoul: Institute of Korean Christianity, 2006.

Jung, Sang-si. "A New Prospect for the Minjung Church Movement as Confluence of the Two Stories." In *Nam-dong Suh and Minjung Theology Today*, edited by the Jukjae Suh Nam-dong Commemoration Committee, 144–56. Seoul: Dongyeon, 2009.

Kang, Won don. "Minjung Theological Adoption of the Minjung Culture Movement." *Theological Thought* 53 (Summer. 1986) 247–86.

———. *A Theology of Matter: A Quest for a Theology Firmly Grounded on Praxis and Materialism*. Seoul: Hanwool, 1992.

Kim, Chang-rak. "Minjung's Struggle for Liberation and Minjung Theology." *Theological Inquiry* 28 (1987) 69–132.

Kim, Eun Soo. "Minjung Theology in Korea: A Critique from a Reformed Theological Perspective." *Japan Christian Review* 64 (1998) 53–65.

Kim, Hiheon. *Minjung and Process: Minjung Theology in Dialogue with Process Thought*. Bern: Peter Lang, 2009.

Kim, Hun-soo. "A Retrospective Essay on the Christian Worldview Movement in the 1980s." In *A Resource Book for the Biblical Worldview*, edited by the Korean Association of Christian Studies, 164–207. Seoul: Korean Association of Christian Studies, 1991.

Kim, Hyun-jin. "The Church Community and the Christian Worldview Movement for the Kingdom of God." *The Christian University* 179 (December 2000). http://jehoooshua.blogspot.com/2012/09/blog-post_804.html.

Kim, Hyun-soo. "The Church Characteristics and the Movement Characteristics." In *Jesus Gone to Galilee*, edited by the Presbyterian Church in the Republic of Korea, Association of Minjung Church Movement, 253–60. Osan, South Korea: Hanshin University Press, 1996.

Kim, Hyoung-hyo. "Regarding the Truth in the Confused Times." *Literature and Thoughts* 31 (April 1975) 375–79.

Kim, Jin-bae. *The Democracy Movement in the 1970s: The Christian Human Rights Movement*. 3 vols. Seoul: National Council of Churches in Korea, Committee of Human Rights, 1987.

Kim, Jin-Ho. "Beyond the Exclusivist Ideology of Theology." *The Era and Minjung Theology* 3 (1996) 4–18.

———. *For a Practical Christianity: the Revolutionary Character of the Jesus Movement*. Seoul: Nathan, 1992.

———. "The Hermeneutics of Ahn Byung-Mu: Focusing on the Concepts of 'Discovery of Internality' and 'Otherness of Minjung.'" In *Reading Minjung Theology in the Twenty-First Century: Selected Writings by Ahn Byung-Mu and Modern Critical Responses*, edited by Yung Suk Kim and Jin-Ho Kim, 13–23. Eugene, OR: Wipf and Stock, 2013.

———. "Minjung as the Subject of History: A Re-Evaluation of the Theory of Minjung in Minjung Theology." *Theological Thought* 80 (Spring 1993) 21–47.

———. "What Is Minjung Theology? – Its Development, Evaluation, and Prospect." *The Era and Minjung Theology* 1 (1994) 24–32.

Kim, Kyong-jae. "A Seed of Grain, Minjung, and the Spirituality of Civil Movements." In *Nam-dong Suh and Minjung Theology Today*, edited by the Jukjae Suh Nam-dong Commemoration Committee, 202–18. Seoul: Dongyeon, 2009.

Kim, Seyoon. "Is 'Minjung Theology' a Christian Theology?" *Calvin Theological Journal* 22/2 (November 1987) 251–74.

Kim, Yong-bock. *Messiah and Minjung: Christ's Solidarity with the People for New Life.* Hong Kong: Christian Conference of Asia, Urban Rural Mission, 1992.

———. "Messiah and the Minjung: Messianic Politics against Political Messianism." In *Minjung and Korean Theology*, edited by the Committee of Theological Study, KNCC, 287–301. Seoul: Korean Theological Study Institute, 1982.

Kim, Young-han. "Problems with Korean Minjung Theology." *Veritas*, 25 November 2009. http://blog.daum.net/gangseo/17958980.

Kim, Young-han, Myong-hyuk Kim, Hyong-ki Lee, and Young-bae Cha. "Forum: An Evaluation of Korean Minjung Theology." *Reformed Thoughts* 3 (1990) 230–76.

Kim, Yung Suk, and Jin-Ho Kim, eds. *Reading Minjung Theology in the Twenty-First Century: Selected Writings by Ahn Byung-Mu and Modern Critical Responses.* Eugene, OR: Wipf and Stock, 2013.

King, Coretta. *My Life with Martin Luther King, Jr.* New York: Avon, 1970. Quoted in John R. W. Stott, *Balanced Christianity*, 51 n. 3. Expanded edition. Downers Grove, IL: InterVarsity, 2014.

Kloosterman, Nelson D. "A Response to 'The Kingdom of God Is Twofold': Natural Law and the Two Kingdoms in the Thought of Herman Bavinck by David VanDrunen." *Calvin Theological Journal* 45/1 (April 2010) 165–76.

Koh, Jik-han. "Personal Spirituality and Transformation Movement." *Gospel and Context* 6 (November/December 1991) 134–39.

Korean Association of Christian Studies, ed. *A Resource Book for the Biblical Worldview.* Seoul: Korean Association of Christian Studies, 1991.

Küster, Volker. *A Protestant Theology of Passion: Korean Minjung Theology Revisited.* Leiden: Brill, 2010.

Kuyper, Abraham. "Common Grace." In *Abraham Kuyper: A Centennial Reader*, edited by James D. Bratt, 165–201. Grand Rapids: Eerdmans, 1998.

———. *Lectures on Calvinism*. Grand Rapids: Eerdmans, 1931, 1981.

———. *Principles of Sacred Theology*. Translated by J. Hendrik De Vries. Grand Rapids: Eerdmans, 1954. Quoted in Richard Mouw, *Abraham Kuyper: A Short and Personal Introduction*, 61 n. 5. Grand Rapids: Eerdmans, 2011.

———. "Sphere Sovereignty." In *Abraham Kuyper: A Centennial Reader*, edited by James D. Bratt, 461–90. Grand Rapids: Eerdmans, 1998.

Lee, Jong-cheol. "From the Christian Worldview Movement to the Civil Society Movement." *Gospel and Context* 13 (November 1992) 124–31.

Lee, Jung Young, ed. *An Emerging Theology in World Perspective: Commentary on Korean Minjung Theology.* Mystic, CT: Twenty-Third, 1988.

———. *Marginality: The Key to Multicultural Theology*. Minneapolis: Augsburg Fortress, 1995.

———. *The Trinity in Asian Perspective*. Nashville: Abingdon, 1996.

Lief, Jason. "Is Neo-Calvinism Calvinism?: A Neo-Calvinist Engagement of Calvin's 'Two-Kingdoms' Doctrine." *Pro Rege* 37/3 (March 2009) 1–12.

Lochman, Jan Milic. *Christ and Prometheus: A Quest for Theological Identity.* Geneva: WCC, 1988.

Longchar, A. Wati. "Teaching Third World Contextual Theologies from Ecumenical Perspective – Tribal/Indigenous People's Theology." *Indian Journal of Theology* 44/1 and 2 (2002) 9–19.

Luther, Martin. *Martin Luther: Selections from His Writings.* Edited by John Dillenberger. New York: Doubleday, 1962.

Marshall, Paul A. *Thine Is the Kingdom: A Biblical Perspective on the Nature of Government and Politics Today*. Grand Rapids: Eerdmans, 1986.

Marshall, Paul A., Sander Griffioen, and Richard J. Mouw, eds. *Stained Glass: Worldviews and Social Science*. Lanham, MD: University Press of America, 1989.

Marx, Karl. *Karl Marx: A Reader*. Edited by Jon Elster. Cambridge: Cambridge University Press, 1986.

McIlhenny, Ryan C., ed. *Kingdom Apart: Engaging the Two Kingdoms Perspectives*. Phillipsburg, NJ: Presbyterian and Reformed, 2012.

Middleton, Richard, and Brian Walsh. *The Transforming Vision: Shaping a Christian World View*. Downers Grove, IL: InterVarsity, 1984.

Min, Anselm K. "From the Theology of Minjoong to the Theology of the Citizen: Reflections on Minjoong Theology in 21st Century Korea." *Journal of Asian and Asian American Theology* 5 (Spring 2002) 11–35.

Moltmann, Jürgen. *The Church in the Power of the Spirit: A Contribution to Messianic Ecclesiology*. Translated by Margaret Kohl. London: SCM, 1977.

———. *Experiences in Theology: Ways and Forms of Christian Theology*. Translated by Margaret Kohl. Minneapolis: Fortress, 2000.

———. *Jesus Christ for Today's World*. Translated by Margaret Kohl. Minneapolis: Fortress, 1994.

Mouw, Richard J. *Abraham Kuyper: A Short and Personal Introduction*. Grand Rapids: Eerdmans, 2011.

———. *Called to Holy Worldliness*. Philadelphia: Fortress, 1980.

———. *Calvinism in the Las Vegas Airport: Making Connections in Today's World*. Grand Rapids: Zondervan, 2004.

———. *The Challenges of Cultural Discipleship: Essays in the Line of Abraham Kuyper*. Grand Rapids: Eerdmans, 2011.

———. *Distorted Truth: What Every Christian Needs to Know about the Battle for the Mind*. New York: Harper & Row, 1989.

———. "Foreword." In *The Calvinistic Concept of Culture*, by Henry R. Van Til. Grand Rapids: Baker Academic, 1959, 2001.

———. *The God Who Commands*. Notre Dame, IN: University of Notre Dame Press, 1990.

———. *He Shines in All That's Fair: Culture and Common Grace*. Grand Rapids: Eerdmans, 2001.

———. *Political Evangelism*. Grand Rapids: Eerdmans, 1973.

———. *Politics and the Biblical Drama*. Grand Rapids: Eerdmans, 1976.

———. *Uncommon Decency: Christian Civility in an Uncivil World*. Revised and expanded edition. Downers Grove, IL: InterVarsity, 2010.

———. "What the Millennialists Have Right." *Perspectives*, 1 December 2009. https://perspectivesjournal.org/blog/2009/12/01/what-the-millennialists-have-right/.

———. *When the Kings Come Marching In: Isaiah and the New Jerusalem*. Grand Rapids: Eerdmans, 1983.

Mullin, Daniel M. "Difficulties Surrounding the Apologetic Use of Worldview in Contemporary Calvinist Scholarship." Th.M. diss., University of Guelph, 2005.

Muller, Richard A. *Dictionary of Latin and Greek Theological Terms: Drawn Principally from Protestant Scholastic Theology*. Grand Rapids: Baker, 1985.

Nathan, Richard, and Insoo Kim. *Both-And: Living the Christ-Centered Life in an Either-Or World*. Downers Grove, IL: InterVarsity, 2013.

BIBLIOGRAPHY

Naugle, David K. *Worldview: The History of a Concept.* Grand Rapids: Eerdmans, 2002.

Niebuhr, H. Richard. *Christ and Culture.* New York: Harper & Row, 1951; San Francisco: HarperSanFrancisco, 2001.

Niebuhr, Reinhold. *Moral Man and Immoral Society: A Study in Ethics and Politics.* New York: Scribner's, 1932; reprint, Louisville: Westminster John Knox, 2001.

O'Donovan, Oliver. *Resurrection and Moral Order: An Outline for Evangelical Ethics.* Grand Rapids: Eerdmans, 1994.

Olson, Roger E. *The Journey of Modern Theology: From Reconstruction to Deconstruction.* Downers Grove, IL: InterVarsity, 2013.

Palmer, Timothy P. "Calvin the Transformationist and the Kingship of Christ." *Pro Rege* 35, no. 3 (March 2007) 32–39.

Presbyterian Church in the Republic of Korea, Association of Minjung Church Movement, ed. *Jesus Gone to Galilee.* Osan, South Korea: Hanshin University Press, 1996.

Rhee, Syngman. "Reconciliation: A Vision of Christian Mission." In *Teaching Mission in a Global Context*, edited by Patricia Lloyd-Sidle and Bonnie Sue Lewis, 69–78. Louisville: Geneva, 2001.

Ryoo, Jang-hyun. "A Study of the Minjung Theological Spirituality." *Theological Forum* 70 (2012) 75–101.

———. "A Theological Review and a Task of the Minjung Church." In *Nam-dong Suh and Minjung Theology Today*, edited by the Jukjae Suh Nam-dong Commemoration Committee, 157–74. Seoul: Dongyeon, 2009.

Ryu, Dae-young. "Theological Background of the Conservative Church's Social Involvement since the 1980s." *Korean Christianity and History* 18 (2003) 37–75.

Schmitt, Carl. *The Leviathan in the State Theory of Thomas Hobbes: Meaning and Failure of a Political Symbol.* Translated by George Schwab and Erna Hilfstein. Chicago: University of Chicago Press, 2008.

Shin, Gi-Wook, Paul Y. Chang, Jung-eun Lee, and Sookyung Kim. "South Korea's Democracy Movement (1970–1993): Stanford Korea Democracy Project Report." Stanford, CA: Shorenstein Asia Pacific Research Center, Stanford University, 2007.

Shin, Won Ha. "Two Models of Social Transformation: A Critical Analysis of the Theological Ethics of John H. Yoder and Richard J. Mouw." PhD diss., Boston University, 1997.

Smith, David L. *Theologies of the 21st Century: Trends in Contemporary Theology.* Eugene, OR: Wipf and Stock, 2014.

Smith, James K. A. "Reforming Public Theology: Two Kingdoms, or Two Cities?" *Calvin Theological Journal* 47/1 (April 2012) 122–37.

Smith, Wilfred Cantwell. *The Faith of Other Men.* New York: New American Library, 1963. Quoted in Jung Young Lee, *The Trinity in Asian Perspective*, 33–34 n. 22, 23. Nashville: Abingdon, 1996.

Stackhouse, Max L. *Public Theology and Political Economy: Christian Stewardship in Modern Society.* Grand Rapids: Eerdmans, 1987.

Stein, Ben. "In Class Warfare, Guess Which Class Is Winning" *New York Times*, 26 November 2006. http://www.nytimes.com/2006/11/26/business/yourmoney/26every.html.

Stott, John R. W. *Balanced Christianity.* Expanded edition. Downers Grove, IL: InterVarsity, 2014.

———, ed. *Making Christ Known: Historic Mission Documents from the Lausanne Movement, 1974–1989.* Grand Rapids: Eerdmans, 1997.

Suh, David Kwang-sun. "Korean Theological Development in the 1970s." In *Minjung Theology: People as the Subjects of History*, edited by the Commission of Theological Concerns of the Christian Conference of Asia, 38–43. Maryknoll, NY: Orbis, 1983.

Suh, Kyung-suk. "The Crisis of Minjung Theology." *Christian Thought* 417 (September 1993) 187–204.

Suh, Nam-dong. "Confluence of the Two Stories." In *Minjung and Korean Theology*, edited by the Committee of Theological Study, KNCC, 237–76. Seoul: Korean Theological Study Institute, 1982.

———. "Envisagement of *Han* and Its Theological Reflection." In *Minjung and Korean Theology*, edited by the Committee of Theological Study, KNCC, 319–47. Seoul: Korean Theological Study Institute, 1982.

———. "Historical References for a Theology of Minjung." In *Minjung Theology: People as the Subjects of History*, edited by the Commission of Theological Concerns of the Christian Conference of Asia, 155–82. Maryknoll, NY: Orbis, 1983.

———. "Missio Dei and Two Stories in Coalescence." In *Asian Contextual Theology for the Third Millennium: Theology of Minjung in Fourth-Eye Formation*, edited by Paul S. Chung, Veli-Matti Karkkainen, and Kyung-Jae Kim, translated by Paul Chung, 51–67. Eugene, OR: Pickwick, 2007.

———. *A Study in Minjung Theology*. Seoul: Hangil Sa, 1983.

———. *A Theology at a Turning Point*. Cheonahn: Korean Theological Study Institute, 1976.

———. "Toward a Theology of Han." In *Minjung Theology: People as the Subjects of History*, edited by the Commission of Theological Concerns of the Christian Conference of Asia, 355–69. Maryknoll, NY: Orbis, 1983.

Sundermeier, Theo. "Missio Dei Today: On the Identity of Christian Mission." *International Review of Mission* 92/4 (2003) 579–87.

Tillich, Paul. *Systematic Theology*. Vol. 1, *Reason and Revelation, Being and God*. Chicago: University of Chicago Press, 1951.

Ucko, Hans. *The People and the People of God: Minjung and Dalit Theology in Interaction with Jewish-Christian Dialogue*. Münster: Lit Verlag, 2002.

VanDrunen, David. "'The Kingship of Christ Is Twofold': Natural Law and the Two Kingdoms in the Thought of Harman Bavinck." *Calvin Theological Journal* 45/1 (April 2010) 147–64.

———. *Living in God's Two Kingdoms: A Biblical Vision for Christianity and Culture*. Wheaton, IL: Crossway, 2010.

———. *Natural Law and the Two Kingdoms: A Study in the Development of Reformed Social Thought*. Grand Rapids: Eerdmans, 2010.

———. "The Two Kingdoms: A Reassessment of the Transformationist Calvin." *Calvin Theological Journal* 4/2 (November 2005) 248–66.

Van Til, Henry R. *The Calvinistic Concept of Culture*. Grand Rapids: Baker, 1959.

Wolters, Albert. *Creation Regained: Biblical Basics for a Reformational Worldview*. Grand Rapids: Eerdmans, 1985.

———. "Dutch Neo-Calvinism: Worldview, Philosophy and Rationality." In *Rationality in the Calvinian Tradition*, edited by Hendrik Hart, Johan Van Der Hoeven, and Nicholas Wolterstorff, 113–31. Christian Studies Today. Lanham, MD: University Press of America, 1983.

———. "Nature and Grace in the Interpretation of Proverbs 31: 10–31." *Calvin Theological Journal* 19/2 (November 1984) 153–66.

———. "Worldview and Textual Criticism in 2 Peter 3:10." *Westminster Theological Journal* 49 (1987) 405–13.

Wolterstorff, Nicholas. "Points of Unease with the Creation Order Tradition." In *An Ethos of Compassion and the Integrity of Creation*, edited by Brian J. Walsh, Hendrik Hart, and Robert E. VanderVennen, 62–66. Lanham, MD: University Press of America, 1995.

———. *Until Justice and Peace Embrace*. Grand Rapids: Eerdmans, 1983.

Yim, Tae-soo. "Minjung Theology toward the Second Reformation." In *Nam-dong Suh and Minjung Theology Today*, edited by the Jukjae Suh Nam-dong Commemoration Committee, 175–201. Seoul: Dongyeon, 2009.

———. *Minjung Theology toward the Second Reformation*. Seoul: Christian Literature Society of Korea, 2002.

———. "Nam-dong Suh's Understanding of Jesus: A New Study on the Understanding of Minjung." In *Is Minjung the Messiah?*, edited by the Institute of Minjung Theology, 111–28. Seoul: Hanwool, 1995.

———. "A New Understanding of Minjung-Messianism." *Madang: International Journal of Contextual Theology in East Asia* 4 (December 2005) 77–90.

Yoder, John H. *The Politics of Jesus: Vicit Agnus Noster*. Grand Rapids: Eerdmans, 1972. Quoted in Richard J. Mouw, *Politics and the Biblical Drama*, 36 n. 19. Grand Rapids: Eerdmans, 1976.

www.ingramcontent.com/pod-product-compliance
Lightning Source LLC
Chambersburg PA
CBHW071501150426
43191CB00009B/1394